WWW.PERCYCHATTEYBOOKS.COM

STORY TELLING

Story Telling Six

February 2018

STORY TELLING

A DIFFERENT SLANT ON LIFE

ISBN 978 9998869 05

Published by

Percychatteybooks Publisher

© Percy W Chattey 2018

Percy W. Chattey has inserted his right under the Copyright, Designs and Patents Act, 1988, to be identified as the author of this work.

SOME ARE LONG
AND SOME ARE TRUE
THERE ARE ONES
THAT ARE SHORT
AND OTHERS ARE BLUE
ALL ARE THOUGHT PROVOKING
WITH FUNNY ONES WORTH A
GIGGLE OR TWO

Percychatteybooks is self-regulating to the contents and reserves the right to alter, change or edit articles and is not responsible for any advice given or knowledge that is imparted and recommendation, guidance or information should be checked on independently before acting on it.

Story Telling Six

As always for my lovely wife Jean, friend and soul mate, who has helped with the editing and all rewrites, also listening to all my ramblings whilst putting these articles together.

My appreciation to the following
Derek Cook for the cover
Richard Seal
Terry Tumbler
All my friends on Social Media who send me their gems.

Contents

My name is Meg, and as in the past I will be your host throughout this creation. But First let me explain the following as it is very important:

The contents and the opinions shown or written here are not necessarily the views of 'Story Telling' or its publisher and are published as articles of interest and amusement only and no offence of any kind religious, racial or political is intended to any person or group of people.

I would also like to add on behalf of Story Telling, in a world where there is so much fake and dishonest stories being bandied around, we cannot guarantee any printed here as being accurate or correct and should be checked on before acting on them.

Let us make a start by this little story about how important it is to have an occupation after retirement!

As we get older we sometimes begin to doubt our ability to "Make a difference" in the world. It is at these times that our hopes are boosted by the remarkable achievements of other "Seniors" who have found the courage to take on challenges that would make many of us wither.

Harold Schlumberg is such a person:

THE FOLLOWING QUOTE IS FROM HAROLD:

"I've often been asked, 'What do you do now that you're retired?'

Well...I'm fortunate to have a chemical engineering background and one of the things I enjoy most is converting beer, wine and whiskey into urine. It's rewarding, uplifting, satisfying and fulfilling. I do it every day and I really enjoy it.."

Harold Is An Inspiration To Us All.
\\\\\\\\\\\\\\\\\\\\\\\\\\\\\\\\\\

A Political Comment

"Anybody may support me when I am right. What I want is someone that will support me when I am wrong." Sir John Macdonald...Canadian Prime Minister.

Want to know about Bitcoins?

If you know what Bitcoins are or are interested in them this is fascinating...as always this is not intended as advice.

A load of monkeys lived near a village.
One day a merchant came to the village to buy these monkeys. He announced that he will buy the monkeys for $100 each.

The villagers thought that this man was mad. They thought how can somebody buy stray monkeys at $100 each?

Still, some people caught some monkeys and gave them to this merchant and he gave them $100 for each monkey.

This news spread like wildfire and people caught more monkeys and sold them to the merchant.

Story Telling Six

After a few days, the merchant announced that he will buy monkeys for $200 each.

The lazy villagers who had not bothered before now ran around to catch the remaining monkeys and they sold the remaining monkeys for $200 each.

Then the merchant announced that he will buy the monkeys for $500 each. The villagers started to lose sleep! ... They caught six or seven monkeys, which was all that was left and got $500 each.

The villagers were waiting anxiously for the next announcement.

Then the merchant announced that he was going home for a week. And when he returns, he will buy the monkeys for $1000 each. He asked his employee to take care of the monkeys he bought.

The employee was alone taking care of all the monkeys in a cage and the merchant went home.

The villagers were very sad as there were no more monkeys left for them to sell at $1000 each.

Then the employee told them that he will sell some monkeys back to them at $700 each secretly.

This news spread like wild fire. Since the merchant will now buy monkeys for $1000 each, there is a $300 profit for each monkey.

The next day, villagers made a queue near the monkey cage. The employee sold all the monkeys at $700 each.

The rich villagers bought monkeys in big lots and the poor ones borrowed money from money lenders and also bought monkeys!
The villagers took care of their monkeys & waited for the merchant to return.

But nobody came so they ran to the employee.
he had already left too !

The villagers then realised that they have bought the useless stray monkeys at $700 each and were unable to sell them!

The Bitcoin will be the next monkey business. It will make a lot of people bankrupt and a few people filthy rich in this monkey business.

Interesting but at Story Telling we only pass this little narrative on.

**

The first microprocessor was not made by Intel. It was actually a classified custom chip used to control the swing wings and flight controls on the first F-14 Tomcats.

**

A NATION THAT FORGETS ITS PAST HAS NO FUTURE.
SIR WINSTON CHURCHILL

The Architectural Designer

After nearly two decades of dealing with various planning departments at differing Local authorities, I still found it difficult to understand the thought process in some of their thinking. The final say over a planning issue lies ultimately with the Planning Committee, however many issues are dealt with by the officers and are nodded through at the committee stage. What always made me smile was when having submitted an application for the redesign of a property the Planning Officer would say it was not acceptable and on asking what was wrong with it, on many occasion the reply has been 'I can't say, you are the designer so it is up to you to put it right.' Perhaps in some incidents they would be helpful.

It was on such an occasion we were asked to change the shape of a long bungalow. It was totally detached and laid back from the road, up a hill at the end of a long drive of about four hundred yards, and was partially obscured by trees. The structure had been built about thirty years previously with a flat roof. Below it was a garage dug into the ground for about four cars. The requirement by the client was to add another storey for sleeping accommodation, and to have a pitched roof.

I pointed out that in my opinion it would not be acceptable to the planning people as it would make the building too high and as it was in the Green Belt we needed to respect the area. I suggested instead of adding another storey with a pitched roof, by saying if we formed the roof on the existing and by making the pitch very steep we could fit the bedrooms within with dormer style windows. With the approval of the client for that type of change I produced finished drawings, which changed the look of the whole structure and transformed a 'bland' looking uninteresting bungalow into a building of character.

I was surprised when the planning officer accepted it as I had expected some difficulty as the property was in an area where getting any form of change is difficult. Because of the Green Belt status the application had to go before the committee...so it was no surprise when I was told the dormer windows were too prominent and I should raise the window seal on them by two hundred millimetres, about eight inches. I almost laughed...200mm - the closest one can see the building is from about half a mile away and at that distance what difference was eight inches going to make.

On another occasion we were instructed by Anglia Windows to modify their warehouse, which they owned in Portishead on the outskirts of Bristol. It was a sizable building on the ground floor with a large opening at each end so lorries could drive through and be unloaded. The whole was on a main road on the outside of a shallow bend, with limited car parking to the front and space so that vehicles could drive round it. The access had been built in a time when lorries weren't as large as the modern counterpart and therefore they had difficulty in manoeuvring through it.

Our instruction was to divide the property into two as Anglia's use of the building had reduced and they wanted to rent out the half they had no use for. In planning terms once any application is made for any reason then the Local Authority have the opportunity to bring any matters which do not comply with current thinking up to date, in this instance the access to the property from the road.

After the survey of the building and the road outside, we went into the design stage. Everything worked out fine although there was some loss of car parking facilities but making the whole site one way traffic the area was adequate for their purpose and complied with the necessary regulations for vehicle access.

To divide the building into two was easy, it was about five metres high at the middle point, which meant building a solid block wall across the centre from the top to the ground. This wall had to have certain design factors, strength so it would not collapse if some clown drove into it, and above all it had to be able to prevent the spread of any fire.

We duly made the planning application and the Local Authority were very happy as we had resolved the problem of the dangerous access to the site, and passed it without query. However, then it had to go to Building Control for their approval. I received a telephone call from a very nice man, and whilst he pointed out everything was acceptable, he thought because of the load on the floor from the block wall then he would like to have a structural engineers report to say that the floor was capable of supporting it.

I had deliberately specified 'Durox' a light weight block, as they are easy to handle and perfectly fireproof and quick in construction terms. At any one position of the floor the weight transferred by the wall would be less than one ton. I listened to what the building inspector had to say and then pointed out to him that Anglia Windows had used forty five ton trucks over the past ten or more years to drive through the warehouse and the floor was not showing any sign of stress. He said no more and passed the application.

<u>Wind</u>

Living in the country, beauty,
peace, tranquility is unreal,
almost surreal for city folk ..
But nature, noticing a cozy
complacency creeping in
around vistas, then steps in
with wild winds whipped up
as if lost at sea, fit to shift,
lift fences, collapse a shed.
Likes to hurl tiles, cut power
to keep us all in our place ..
See if we still love the stars
with a tree lying on our car.

Copyright Richard Seal 2017

**

**One man with convictions will
overwhelm a hundred who only have
opinions.
Sir Winston Churchill**

The Teacher

After being interviewed by the school administration, the prospective teacher said:

"Let me see if I've got this right.

You want me to go into that room with all those kids, correct their disruptive behaviour, observe them for signs of abuse, monitor their dress habits, censor their T-shirt messages and instil in them a love for learning.

You want me to check their backpacks for weapons, wage war on drugs and sexually transmitted diseases, and raise their sense of self esteem and personal pride.

You want me to teach them patriotism and good citizenship, sportsmanship and fair play, and how to register to vote, balance a chequebook, and apply for a job.

You want me to check their heads for lice, recognise signs of antisocial behaviour, and ensure that they all pass their final exams.

You also want me to provide them with an equal education regardless of their handicaps, and communicate regularly with their parents in English,

Arabic or any other language, by letter, telephone, newsletter, and report card.

You want me to do all this with a piece of chalk, a blackboard, a bulletin board, a few books, a big smile, and a starting salary that qualifies me for "New Start."

You want me to do all this, and then you tell me...I CAN'T wear a necklace with a little cross, mention God, or say "Merry Christmas" because <u>someone</u> might take offence? Well, you know what you can do with your job........

\\\

Emergency Calls to 911

Dispatcher: 9-1-1 What is your emergency?
Caller: I heard what sounded like gunshots coming from the brown house on the corner.
Dispatcher: Do you have an address?
Caller: No, I have on a blouse and slacks, why?

Dispatcher: 9-1-1, **Caller:** Yeah, I'm having trouble breathing. I'm all out of breath. Darn...I think I'm going to pass out. **Dispatcher:** Sir, where are you calling from?
Caller: I'm at a pay phone. North and Foster.
Dispatcher: Sir, an ambulance is on the way. Are you an asthmatic? **Caller:** No
Dispatcher: What were you doing before you started having trouble breathing? **Caller:** Running from the Police.

Dispatcher: 9-1-1 What is your emergency?
Caller: Someone broke into my house and took a bite out of my ham and cheese sandwich .
Dispatcher: 9-1-1 What is the nature of your emergency?
Caller: I'm trying to reach nine eleven but my phone doesn't have an eleven on it.
Dispatcher: This is nine eleven.
Caller: I thought you just said it was nine-one-one
Dispatcher: Yes, ma'am nine-one-one and nine-eleven are the same thing.
Caller: Honey, I may be old, but I'm not stupid.

**

The Shave!

An old cowboy walks into a barbershop in Red Lodge, Montana for a shave and a haircut. He tells the barber he can't get all his whiskers off because his cheeks are wrinkled from age.

The barber gets a little wooden ball from a cup on the shelf and tells the old cowboy to put it inside his cheek to spread out the skin. When he's finished, the old cowboy tells the barber that was the cleanest shave he'd had in years, but he wanted to know what would have happened if he had accidentally swallowed the little ball..

The barber replied, "Just bring it back in a couple of days like everyone else does".

**

1993 Grand National

The **1993 Grand National** was scheduled on 3 April 1993 to be the 147th running of the horse race, held annually at Aintree Racecourse near Liverpool, England. The meeting had been beset by problems before the race. Fifteen animal rights protesters had invaded the course near the first fence resulting in a delayed start.

The first false start was caused by several riders becoming tangled in the starting tape. Starter Keith Brown, who was officiating his last National before retirement, waved his red recall flag and a second official, Ken Evans, who was situated 100 yards further down the track, in turn signaled to the leading runners to turn around.

Story Telling Six

At the second attempt, the tape became tangled again around the neck of jockey Richard Dunwoody and Brown called another false start. However, this time his recall flag did not unfurl as he waved it. As a result, 30 of the 39 riders set off around the track, oblivious to the recall.

The BBC's lead commentator Peter O'Sullevan describes the second false start.

"And they're away — oh, and once again the tape has snagged, and it's a recall...It was caught round Richard Dunwoody's neck, the tape. And they've been recalled — but the majority don't realise that it is a recall! They're going down to jump the first, they're going to!"

Officials, trainers and the crowd tried desperately to halt the race, but the majority of the field continued racing. Commentator Peter O'Sullevan declared the unfolding events "the greatest disaster in the history of the Grand National".

Peter O'Sullevan describes the climax of the 'race'.

"So as they race up to the line, in the National that surely isn't, Esha Ness is the winner, second is Cahervillahow, third is Romany King, four The Committee, five is Givus A Buck. Then comes On The Other Hand and Laura's Beau and they are the only ones to have completed in the race that surely never was."

Initially there was confusion as to what would happen next. Keith Brown, the race starter, was interviewed briefly by the BBC and alluded to the possibility that the nine jockeys who noticed and obeyed his recall could be eligible to take part in a re-run. Several jockeys said that they thought the officials attempting to stop them were actually protestors Esha Ness's jockey John White said of the latter stages of the race: "I could see there were only a few horses around, but I thought the others had fallen or something."

The Jockey Club later declared the race void, ruled out any re-running of it, and launched an inquiry. Bookmakers were forced to refund an estimated £75 million in bets staked.

**

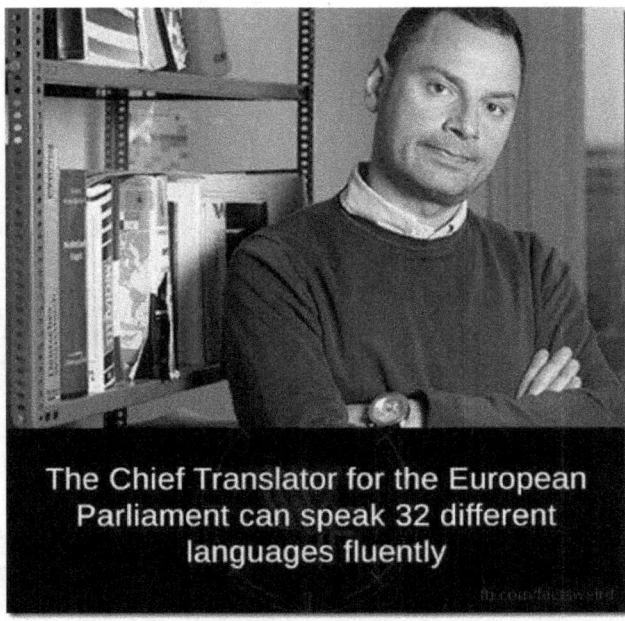

The Chief Translator for the European Parliament can speak 32 different languages fluently

A lot is said about Drinking and Driving but this story sums it up

I was walking around in a Big Bazaar store shopping, when I saw a Cashier talking to a boy who couldn't have been more than 5 or 6 years old..

The Cashier said, 'I'm sorry, but you don't have enough money to buy this doll". Then the little boy turned to the cashier and asked: "Are you sure I don't have enough money?"

The cashier counted his cash once again and replied: "You know that you don't have enough money to buy the doll, my dear." The little boy was still holding the doll in his hand.

Finally, I walked toward him and I asked him who he wished to give this doll to. 'It's the doll that my sister loved most and wanted so much . I wanted to Gift her for her BIRTHDAY.

I have to give the doll to my mommy so that she can give it to my sister when she goes there.' His eyes were so sad while saying this. 'My Sister has gone to be with God.. Daddy says that Mommy is going to see God very soon too, so I thought that she could take the doll with her to give it to my sister..."

Story Telling Six

My heart nearly stopped. The little boy looked up at me and said: 'I told daddy to tell mommy not to go yet. I need her to wait until I come back from the mall.' Then he showed me a very nice photo of him where he was laughing. He then told me 'I want mommy to take my picture with her so my sister won't forget me.' 'I love my mommy and I wish she doesn't have to leave me, but daddy says that she has to go to be with my little sister.' Then he looked again at the doll with sad eyes, very quietly..

I quickly reached for my wallet and said to the boy. 'Suppose we check again, just in case you do have enough money for the doll?"

'OK' he said, 'I hope I do have enough.' I added some of my money to his without him seeing and we started to count it. There was enough for the doll and even some spare money.

The little boy said: 'Thank you God for giving me enough money!'

Then he looked at me and added, 'I asked last night before I went to sleep for God to make sure I had enough money to buy this doll, so that mommy could give It to my sister. He heard me!" 'I also wanted to have enough money to buy a white rose for my mommy, but I didn't dare to ask God for too much. But He gave me enough to buy the doll and a white rose. My mommy loves white roses.'

I finished my shopping in a totally different state from when I started. I couldn't get the little boy out of my mind.

Then I remembered a local newspaper article two days ago, which mentioned a drunk man in a truck, who hit a car occupied by a young woman and a little girl. The little girl died right away, and the mother was left in a critical state. The family had to decide whether to pull the plug on the life-sustaining machine, because the young woman would not be able to recover from the coma. Was this the family of the little boy?

Two days after this encounter with the little boy, I read in the newspaper that the young woman had passed away...I couldn't stop myself as I bought a bunch of white roses. I went to the funeral home where the body of the young woman was exposed for people to see and make last wishes before her burial.

She was there, in her coffin, holding a beautiful white rose in her hand with the photo of the little boy and the doll placed over her chest. I left the place, teary-eyed, feeling that my life had been changed for ever...The love that little boy had for his mother and his sister is still, to this day, hard to imagine. And in a fraction of a second, a drunk driver had taken all this away from him.

Please <u>DO NOT DRINK & DRIVE.</u>

The Weather Forecast Dec 2017.

This is from a weather forecaster on television and she is describing it as very bad with snow and ice. And how the roads weren't moving. She went on to say "The M62 is running nicely" *She did not say what happened when it ran out of breath! Perhaps roads don't run out of breath.*

She continued "The RAC said "they had a breakdown every 30 seconds'." You would think they would be certain their vehicles didn't break down.

\\\\\\\\\\\\\\\\\\\\\\\\\\\\\\\\\\

"The reason there are so few female politicians is that it is too much trouble to put makeup on two faces"
     Maureen Murphy (Politician)

\\\\\\\\\\\\\\\\\\\\\\\\\\\\\\\\\\

Did you Know Line dancing was started by women waiting for the Bathroom

---

This is just so English!!!

One of the English national daily newspapers asked readers: "What does it mean to be English?" Some of the emails were hilarious but this one from a chap in Switzerland stood out:

"Being English is about driving in a German car to an Irish pub for a Belgian beer, and then going home, grabbing an Indian curry or a Turkish kebab on the way, to sit on Swedish furniture and watch American or Australian shows on a Japanese or Korean TV, which will soon be powered by a Chinese nuclear power station."

And the most English thing of all? .... "Suspicion of anything foreign."

\\\\\\\\\\\\\\\\\\\\\\\\\\\\\\\

"There are two kinds of people, those who do the work and those who take the credit. Try and be in the first group there is less competition there." Indire Gandhi

---

The Dutch Uncle

A doctor of great eminence had a gift for curing heartache. He was a psychologist and psychiatrist who worshiped God. For many years he was a potent and inspiring force in a great neurological institution and now in retirement is called by the medical profession a saint.

The nervous wrecks and neurotics whom he salvaged, the coward he heartened, all could have had the benefit of modern hospital techniques. But he let others practise analysis, group therapy and shock treatments. His way was to speak to them like a Dutch uncle. "You!" He often told them, "Are the sole cause of your condition – and only you can cure yourself."

The doctor would then go on to say "More diseases are caused by a malevolent point of view than by germs. Our bodies have a natural resistance to microbes but the defence can be broken down by grudges and hates, even little ones, if we have enough of them. Hippocrates, the father of medicine, was right when he said 'Anger and fear breed a poison in the blood. A perfect healthy person can be overcome by vengeful ideas and eventually be crippled by arthritis or rheumatism for the rest of their lives.

Story Telling Six

Common sense and the knack of seeing things as they are is our protection. There is an old prayer which runs 'God grant me the courage to change the things I can change, the serenity to accept the things I cannot change, and the wisdom to know the difference.'

With such a spirit of good will a man or woman can do more than avoid the penalties of malevolence; he or she can help themselves to make a success of their lives. One of the best parables the doctor would frequently tell was the story of the young violinist:

'At an early age Frances toured the hinterland of the United States with her own chamber music quartet. Suddenly her widowed father became paralysed, she gave up her tour to nurse and comfort him. At his death two years later, she took what was left of her savings and went to New York. After months of canvassing the studios she realised the city was full of aspiring young violinists. That was when Frances recalled her fathers wise words, 'Never quail before facts. Look at the difficulty and tell yourself what has to be done.'

So with her remaining two hundred dollars she entered a business college to learn shorthand and typing. Finishing near to the top of the class she still could not find work.

Story Telling Six

The depression was on and there were too many secretaries. One Sunday she put this advertisement in a New York classified column: 'I can't get a job without experience. And I can't get experience without a job. That is why I will work four weeks for you without pay – and then leave you. You have no obligation whatsoever. And I am good!' She received more than a thousand replies, picked three of the best and made arrangements with them. She earned good money for the rest of her career and finished working at the White House during President Roosevelt's presidency.

To acquire the right point of view - and hold on to it – is not easy. Somehow we look at the wrong thing in the wrong way. There is the story of the young soldier wounded in the battle of The Bulge. As he came out of the ether on the operating table, the army surgeon spoke to him tenderly: 'You're going to be alright son. The only bad part is you have lost a leg.'
'Nuts!' said the soldier. 'I didn't lose it I gave it away.' Because he chose to look at in that way the rest of his life would be richer, without bitterness or resentment he could start again to shape his future.

Resentment grows by feeling injured feelings. In the grip of hostility a person can lie awake at night, making out a plausible case against his enemy reading mean motives into another's word or deed. Such a state of mind is a robber of sleep; it rouses the victim without appetite and sends him into the day with a chip on his shoulder and goads him on to quarrel.

If you think you're badly treated by your wife or husband then the doctor will tell you the famous story of Kepler the astronomer. Having made a failure of his first marriage, he decided his second wife must be chosen scientifically. First he made a list of the women he considered eligible, then he wrote on one side of their names their good qualities and on the other side their bad ones. Mathematically he chose the lady with the most good qualities

Keplers second marriage was a worst failure than the first and the scientist declared that the whole problem was insoluble. But never once did he think of listing his bad qualities. Either marriage might have been a success if he had looked into his own heart for the remedies.

And finally he said, when in pain don't think of the pain but of life without it, the hurt will then be far less intense and will go away.

£280,000 Mortgage

This was voted best joke for 2013...it is worth repeating.

For his birthday, little Joseph asked for a 10-speed bicycle. His father said, 'Son, we'd give you one, but the mortgage on this house is. £280,000 and your mothers' just lost her job. There's no way we can afford it.'

The next day the father saw little Joseph heading out the front door with a suitcase. So he asked, 'Son, where are you going?' Little Joseph told him, 'I was walking past your room last night and heard you telling mum you were pulling out. Then I heard her tell you to wait because she was coming too. So I am off if you think I'm staying here by myself with a £280,000 mortgage and no bike!

\\\

Politics is supposed to be the second oldest profession. I have come to realise that it bears a very close resemblance to the first. Ronald Reagan (US President).

Air Travel

As the year two thousand and seventeen disappears behind us, it will no doubt be remembered in the main for the appalling weather, which in some cases is continuing into this year. The unusual deadly freezing temperatures that have spread across North East America are just an example; can we believe the experts when they tell us it is the start of a new ice age? It was not too long ago we were told about the horrors of 'global warming', a phrase which was constantly repeated, with World Leaders holding summits to discuss how to combat it.

This transformed, I am not certain when, but instead of GW we are now told about 'climate change'. A lovely phrase! It has no meaning because the perpetrators of it cannot be wrong...if it gets colder they are right and if on the other hand the opposite happens then they are still right. We must not forget other experts who understand the science of looking back on the World history, and they will argue that any change is only an adjustment in the weather pattern and has been going on since the start of time.

One thing we are very certain about and that is our cities are killing people through the pollution that has taken place, because of our love of travelling and the use of the motor car and similar modes of transport. It is a repeat of what happened in the forties and the fifties when the use of burning coal to heat our homes brought thick smog especially in the autumn. If you have never experienced it let me explain. The smoke from the coal fires was full of soot and when it mixed with the cold damp air it became very difficult to breathe, and your face would be covered in black specks especially around your nose. The difference is then you could see it...now it is a silent killer as the fumes from a combustion engine are not so obvious.

Where we live in South East Spain the skies on most days are clear and a beautiful pastel blue. As we are sitting by the pool looking at the wonderland around us in the warmth of the sun, high above us two to three hundred people are sitting in a tin box being taken somewhere. No doubt, they in the main will be full of excitement and as they gaze out of the window of the flying machine they will see vapour pouring off the wing edges. Probably totally meaningless to them as that is what happens and they have seen it before.

We on the ground look skywards and watch this tiny speck five or six miles above us making its way across the heavens until it disappears over the horizon. It has gone but some of it is still there behind it, for it has left a long stream of water vapour mixed with burnt engine fuel. As the day progresses this vapour spreads into a long wide cloud; and as more and more tin boxes cross the sky then each of them leaves a similar trail, and like the others it will grow, effectually blotting out the blue.

I have just gone into 'Flightradar 24' an App which tracks every aircraft in the air and as I write there are ten thousand planes flying around the world. As most flights only take two or three hours it is difficult to calculate how many planes are taking off and flying on a daily basis. Each in its own way leaving behind it burnt fuel and high in the sky water vapour, which eventually finds it way downwards...is that why we are having so many rain storms? So perhaps the pundits are right climate change is about how we treat the environment, but who is brave enough to tell the people they can no longer fly!!!

www.percychatteybooks.com

**

Eating Out

**For the greatest lovers
of fine food, eating out
will always be such a joy.
Whether tackling salad,
soup or peppered steak
make no mistake this lad
will relish it with pleasure,
treasure every last slice
of cake, and take his time
finishing a glass of wine,
lingering long with glee
over an Irish coffee.**

Copyright Richard Seal 2017

**

**There is nothing government can give you that it hasn't taken from you in the first place.
Sir Winston Churchill**

Two Hours of Fun!

The day had started bright with the sun sliding up the sky in the East. Bob yawned as he slipped out of bed to join his young wife Gill at the window. She was looking out watching at the new light of the day as it spread across their garden, still damp from a previous very heavy downpour of rain laced with hail stones. They were pleased everything seemed to have changed and looked like it was going to be a nice day, as that evening they had planned the long trip into town to see a stage show of one of their favourite artists.

The travelling decision had been made a long time previously in that they would take the bus, which regularly stopped at the end of their road, instead of worrying about parking the car in what was a very busy part of the city. And as Bob said, that would allow him to have a drink. As the afternoon wore on, dark clouds gathered in the sky with a slight breeze blowing the brown and yellow leaves around that had fallen from the trees, now that summer had given way to the fall and the nights were starting to close in.

They were both a little disappointed at the change, especially as the rain spots were developing into a drizzle. Now it was time to leave for their adventure into town,

with a smile on her face Gill went to the wardrobe and
came back holding two coats, slipping her arms through the
sleeves of one of them and with a grin passed her husband
the other, as he reached for the keys to the car. Still
smiling and with eyes sparkling, she gently took his hand
away from them saying, "No, no sweet, we agreed we would
go by bus." He shrugged his shoulder and turned towards
the door.

They held each other's hand as they shut the garden gate.
Both had big grins on their faces and their eyes were
playing games with each others. They continued to hold
hands as they practically skipped down the road laughing,
ignoring the wind and the rain that had got a little
stronger.

There was a small line of people waiting for the trip into
town and they joined the end of it. The conversation
between them was centred around the singing star they
were due to see at the old Theatre. It was a place full of
mature memories, not only for them but also others, of
times long since past as it was built in the late eighteen
hundreds

.

They were busy in their own conversation, giggling at their
silly jokes and hardly noticing the others in the queue...until
they started to move away from the kerb. Bob looked from

his wife to see the bus bearing down on them and then he noticed the water in the gutter and quickly and roughly pulled Gill away from the kerb as the large wheels ploughed into it throwing water across the pavement. At first Gill was shocked at his actions, then she realised what he had saved her from and gave him a quick peck on the cheek.

Although Bob had remarked how cold the bus was on more than one occasion, they were still in good spirits when they finally arrived at their destination only to find the means of transport did not stop outside the theatre but a little way from it. When he grumbled about the walk, Gill quickly pointed out to him that if they had taken the car it would have been a lot further from the car park, for a moment he pulled a face and they quickly resumed their light hearted banter.

It started to rain more heavily before they had reached the foyer of the premises, they were still laughing as they entered through the swing doors having had to wait for a short period while other people moved in front of them. On entering they were a little disappointed, for in their minds it would be warmer but as they slipped out of their coats, shaking the article to remove the worst of the water from them, they realised it was just as cold inside as it was out.

The line shuffled forward to the cash desk where they

produced their booking number and in exchange received tickets so they could enter the auditorium. But first the walk up the wide stairway to take them up to the circle. Suddenly she was aware that he was not responding so she asked. "You are quiet...is something the matter?"

"Sorry I was looking at the state of the paintwork and just wondering how long since it had been decorated."

For the first time Gill was aware of the old decor on the stairway in need of being improved. Following her husband's line of sight to where he had been looking, she felt a little down seeing peeling paint work and poorly maintained stairs. She held his arm tightly saying "It will be fine when we get to our seats."

They continued climbing up the stairs, being jostled by others as they made their way quickly up to the Circle with Bob murmuring "I hope its bloody warmer than this stairway, there is a draught coming from somewhere."

On entering the Auditorium the pair were welcomed by a smartly dressed attendant in a stylish burgundy uniform, who with a smile on her face directed then to their seats, which were in the middle of a row on the far side of the entrance. Bob was still feeling cold and remarked in a hurt voice that he thought they had booked seats which were nearer the centre of the theatre, but agreed it was a little warmer. Nevertheless, when they sat down with empty seats in front of them they could see the stage clearly.

The premises started to fill up as interim music spread through the vast space. Gill feeling very happy and looking forward to the show held his hand tightly and smiling asked if he was okay. "Did you see where the loo was, I think I should go before the show starts?" she looked at him in surprise saying I think it is somewhere at the back. He was getting to his feet and was asking the other people in the seats next to him to excuse him. They shuffled to their feet with a sickly grin on their faces.

He struggled up the steps trying to avoid the people coming down all anxious to find their places. He found the door to the facilities he wanted only to find he had to go down more steps in an unheated corridor and the amenities were no better as he once more queued to take his turn. As he did so he could hear the orchestra was starting and a voice announcing the show would start in five minutes.

Arriving back in the hall he was surprised to find the lights had been lowered and in the dim glow he made his way back to his seat. A comedian had come on the stage and was starting to go through his routine. Bob arrived at the end of the row of seats. "Excuse me!" The man sitting on the outside seat glared at him and someone in the row behind said "Be quiet."

After some kerfuffle, with people standing up and the seat making a muffled bang as the occupier sat down, he arrived at his position with his wife who was also telling him to be quiet. To his total disappointment a person had sat in the row in front of him, a tall man whose head and shoulders blocked out most of his view of the centre of the stage, but by leaning from side to side he managed to see what was happening.

They both enjoyed the first half of the performance and at the interval discovered if they wanted refreshment then they would have to go to the floor below from where they were seated. They joined the steady flow of people making their way to the stairway. Both were laughing and remarking on the performance they had witnessed.

There were deep lines of people around the bar, most with sombre faces as they waited their turn to be served. Bob had joined the throng as people on all sides were pushing gently forward. He managed to get to the bar, which was soaked in spilt drinks, just as the booming voice of the announcer was telling everyone that there were five minutes remaining before the show resumed.

Story Telling Six

With a wet sleeve on his jacket, where he had leant on the counter whilst paying an excessive amount of money for the small plastic container with a minuscule drink, which he now held trying not to squeeze the thin side of it. He returned to his wife and with a sickly smile handed her the tipple and carrying it and trying not to spill the contents they returned to their seats back up the scruffy staircase.

A standing ovation by the spectators ended the show with everyone clapping as the backing chorus, holding hands in a long line took a bow whilst the star of the show skipped on to the stage waving his hands in the air nodding and clapping at the same time.

Retrieving their coats from under the seats they lifted them up brushing them down as they did so to remove the fluff that had accumulated on the floor. They were still laughing at some of the jokes the comedian had told as they joined the throng to exit the building.

Reaching the bottom of the stairs and entering the foyer they were horrified to see it was pouring heavily with rain which was being lashed around by a strong wind. People were hesitating at the door before going through it out into the appalling weather. They followed running down the pavement to the bus stop, with the water starting to run down their necks as the coats they were wearing had little protection at the collar against what nature was doing.

It had been a long wait but eventually a bus came along and they climbed aboard...looking at each other, and much to the surprise of the other passengers they burst out into fits of deep laughter, as the water dripped from their coats.   *Copyright Percychatteybooks*

**

Big Day

**Big day tomorrow, cannot sleep,
too anxious now for counting sheep;
late night becomes the early hours
tries soothing thoughts of fruit and flowers.
Still wide awake at ten to five
she beats the birds in coming alive.
Seeing traces of the morning light
helps body to give up the fight,
sleep comes at last with inner calm
moments before the six thirty alarm ...**
Copyright Richard Seal 2017

**

Politics, a strife of interest masquerading as a contest of principles. Ambrose Piece (Journalist)

Negativity

A woman was at her hairdresser's getting her hair styled
for a trip to Rome with her husband.. She mentioned the
trip to the hairdresser, who responded:
" Rome ? Why would anyone want to go there? It's
crowded and dirty. You're crazy to go to Rome . So, how
are you getting there?"
"We're taking Continental," was the reply. "We got a
great rate!"
**"Continental?" exclaimed the hairdresser. "That's a
terrible airline.**
Their planes are old, their flight attendants are ugly, and
they're always late. So, where are you staying in Rome ?"
"We'll be at this exclusive little place over on
Rome's Tiber River called Teste."
"Don't go any further. I know that place. Everybody thinks
it's going to be something special and exclusive, but it's
really a dump."
"We're going to go to see the Vatican and maybe get to see
the Pope."
"That's rich," laughed the hairdresser. "You and a million
other people trying to see him. He'll look the size of an
ant.
Boy, good luck on this lousy trip of yours. You're going to
need it."
A month later, the woman again came in for a hairdo.
The hairdresser asked her about her trip to Rome .

"It was wonderful," explained the woman, "not only were we on time in one of Continental's brand new planes, but it was overbooked, and they bumped us up to first class. The food and wine were wonderful, and I had a handsome 28-year-old steward who waited on me hand and foot. And the hotel was great! They'd just finished a $5 million remodeling job, and now it's a jewel, the finest hotel in the city.

They, too, were overbooked, so they apologized and gave us their owner's suite at no extra charge!"

"Well," muttered the hairdresser, "that's all well and good, but I know you didn't get to see the Pope"

"Actually, we were quite lucky, because as we toured the Vatican , a Swiss Guard tapped me on the shoulder, and explained that the Pope likes to meet some of the visitors, and if I'd be so kind as to step into his private room and wait, the Pope would personally greet me. Sure enough, five minutes later, the Pope walked through the door and shook my hand! I knelt down and he spoke a few words to me.."

"Oh, really! What'd he say?"

He said: "Who did *THAT* to your hair?"

**

A lie gets half way round the world before the truth gets its pants on.
Sir Winston Churchill

CASA FUENTELARGO
A beautiful spacious detached Holiday Home in the Spanish countryside.

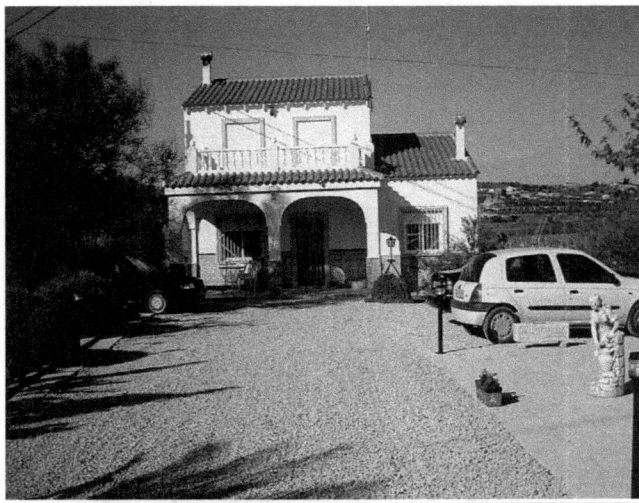

This lovely villa has plenty of space to enjoy the warm weather and sleeps nine people in five bedrooms, it is available for holiday rentals with the use of a private 8 x 4 metre swimming pool, and other games for your enjoyment.

The Pool and Dart Board

Further details at
www.fuentelargo.com

Casa FuenteLargo has received very high reviews on Trip Advisor and Booking.com

Laughing Sailor

Mike loved beach holidays as a child, enjoying fish and chips, donkey rides, games of cards on frequent wet days, swimming whilst the red flag flew, and even the sand sticking to his wet flesh. However, going to amusement arcades was his favourite pastime by far. Unable to resist the lure of a nostalgic seaside trip, Mike returns to Scarthorpe thirty years after his last visit to check out the resort before considering a holiday there with his own family. He is overjoyed to find that Fun Land, his favourite arcade, is still here ...

He gazes down at the Penny Falls machine, his mind ablaze with nineteen seventies joy and images of red, green and orange flashing lights .. In his mind he can still hear the dink chinking of some of the coins dropping, while others hang suspended with purple tubes of fizzy sweets and plastic watches. However, the glass is cold now against his hands, the machine has long since been switched off and plunged into eternal darkness. A single penny lies in the tray below.

As a child he was robbed in this arcade by a particular one-armed bandit. It had swallowed all his pocket money, the last coin getting stuck in the unyielding slot. However, two years later he had exacted revenge on the same machine, which was now faulty and paying out for free. He had emptied it without mercy, before going on to lose all his winnings to its heartless neighbour. Thereafter Mike has been happy playing pinball; all love of gambling gone, he never again desires to see three plums.

Suddenly Mike stands frozen in thrilled chill shock and awe, at this moment realising that he must return and share this place with his children: The same Laughing Sailor is still grinning

back at Mike after all these years, daring him to drop a coin in the slot again. The figure would always insist that you stared in horror at his face, before joining him awhile in a dreadful place: A tight glass box without air or escape, where terror took a painted shape...
Richard Seal Copyright 2017

**

First Recorded Cuppa
(The Tea Break)

City, London. It is thought that the first tea may have been imported into Britain in about 1650, by the Dutch East India Company. But the earliest record we have of any British person taking a cuppa dates from September 25 1660: the man enjoying the beverage was none other than Samuel Pepys, follower of fashion. Having spent time at the office discussing international politics he notes: "And afterwards I did send for a cup of tee (a China drink) of which I never had drank before." So he may have established that British institution the tea break.

**

Governments first duty is to protect the people not to run their lives. Ronald Reagan (US President)

Tea Break

At four o'clock on wet Sunday afternoons he often recalls how, as children, all fun activities had to be put on hold at this time for afternoon tea. No-one ever moaned when faced with jam and cream scones; it never seemed boring watching tea leaves being strained, although it was hard to refrain from crushing sugar lumps into grains.

Sometimes Grandma was there, always equipped with a variety of handkerchiefs' which seemed so refined. She refused to stoop to using disposable tissues - God forbid! Over tea, she scowled if anyone should dare to suggest using a paper napkin. Only linen ones, neatly folded, would suffice. She firmly believed that no-one should need asking twice, anything less than the best was not nice.

Mum had always warmed her favourite tea pot in advance, then it was cosy-clad, somehow smug after the pouring. It was badly cracked one day, dropped by his brother. Seeing the terrible toll that the accident had taken on the face of her youngest son, who had been trying to help with the washing up, mum said with a grin how glad she was to have a special place to keep all her precious things in.

All his family, just like that tea set, are long gone. He is the last one, sharing sepia scenes with the young Queen, pictured a few years after the war, smiling on the special coasters which were kept aside for best, and are still in the cupboard drawer.

Copyright Richard Seal 2017

A Wonderful Poem by the late Spike Milligan

Smiling is infectious
You catch it like the flu

When someone smiled at me today
I started smiling too

I walked around the corner
And someone saw me grin

When he smiled I realised
I had passed it on to him

I thought about the smile
And then realised its worth

A single smile like mine
Could travel around the earth

So if you feel a smile begin
Don't leave it undetected

Start an epidemic
And get the world infected.

The First Boat Race
on the River Thames

Coxed eight rowing had been popular at the University of Oxford for a number of years before a club was established at the University of Cambridge around 1827. At a meeting of the Cambridge University Boat Club in February 1829, it was decided to challenge Oxford "to row a match at or near London, each in an eight-oared boat during the ensuing Easter vacation".[J] The race was deferred to the summer, as rowing did not start at Oxford until after Easter, and scheduled for 10 June 1829 for a prize of 500 guineas. During the pre-race betting, Cambridge were the favourites to win the race.

Oxford wore a dark blue check outfit for the race, while Cambridge wore white with pink waistbands. The two boats were said to be "very handsome, and wrought in a superior style of workmanship" by *The Morning Post*; Oxford's green boat was built by Stephen Davies and Isaac King of Oxford, and was slightly the shorter, measuring 44 feet (13 m). Cambridge's pink boat was 18 inches (0.46 m) longer, and built by Searle of Westminster.[6][7] The umpires for the race were Mr. Cyril Page (for Oxford) and Mr John Stuart Roupell (for Cambridge). Should the umpires disagree about any aspect of the race, they had recourse to consult the referee, whose name was not recorded.

The course of the inaugural Boat Race started at Hambleden Lock and ended at Henley Bridge. The course for the race was a 2.25-mile (3.62 km) stretch of the River Thames between Hambleden Lock and Henley Bridge. Cambridge won the toss and elected to start on the Berkshire side of the river, handing the Buckinghamshire side to Oxford. According to the author William Fisher MacMichael, "it was as fine a day as our climate allows a June day to be." The race had originally been scheduled to start at 6:00 p.m. but this was altered to 7:00 p.m. and was further delayed. Upon the start of the race, by which time around 20,000 people were reckoned to be in attendance to watch, the Oxford boat was steered close to the Cambridge boat, forcing it to row close to the shore. This drew complaints from the Cambridge crew, who insisted that the race be restarted. The Oxford crew relented, and the race began for the second time at 7:55 p.m. In the early stages of the race, the two crews were evenly matched, but after they passed an island in the river, Oxford drew ahead.

Once they had passed the island, and were in the main flow of the river, the Oxford crew demonstrated their strength. *The Morning Post* report of the race records that both crews "put out the strength of their arms in excellent style", and although the Cambridge boat maintained a higher stroke rate, Oxford maintained their lead throughout the rest of the race. Their margin of victory is variously reported as being between two and four lengths (although is recorded officially as "easily"), in a time reported variously between 14 minutes and 14 minutes 30 seconds.

**

Stay away from negative people they have a problem for every solution. Albert Einstein.

<u>*Sometimes it is important to Pay Attention*</u>

An attractive blonde arrived at the casino. She seemed a little intoxicated and bet twenty thousand Euros in a single roll of the dice.

She said, "I hope you don't mind, but I feel much luckier when I'm completely nude."

With that, she stripped from the neck down, rolled the dice and yelled, "Come on, baby, Mama needs new clothes!"

As the dice came to a stop, she jumped up and down and squealed. "Yes! Yes! I won, I won!" She hugged each of the dealers, picked up her winnings and her clothes and quickly departed.

The dealers stared at each other dumbfounded. Finally, one of them asked, "What did she roll?"

The other answered,

"I don't know - I thought you were watching."

**

We learn from experience that men never learn anything from experience.

George Bernard Shaw.

**

Action speaks louder than words, but not nearly as often. Mark Twain

How to Tell the Sex of a Fly

A woman walked into the kitchen to find her
Husband standing around with a fly swatter
"What are you doing?" She asked.
"Hunting Flies" He responded.
"Oh. ! Killing any?" She asked.
"Yep, 3 males, 2 Females," he replied.
Intrigued, she looked at him questionably .
"How can you tell them apart?"
He looked at her and smiled, 3 were on a beer can, 2
were on the phone.

\\\\\\\\\\\\\\\\\\\\\\\\\\\\\\\\\\\\\

The British Army servicing for fifteen pounder guns
was revised following the Second World War.
After the showing of a training film which
revealed that Gunner Number 6 stood smartly to
attention throughout the whole exercise without
performing a single operation.
After lengthy inquiries, puzzled staff officers finally
found a veteran of the Boer War who could
explain the function of gunner G6.
He remembered at that time he used to hold the
horses.

Farmers Maths

A good math's problem for those of us who learned numbers, before the current method of teaching came into existence

A farmer died leaving his 17 horses to his three sons. When his sons opened up the Will it read:
My eldest son should get 1/2 (half) of total horses;
My middle son should be given 1/3rd (one-third) of the total horses;
My youngest son should be given 1/9th (one-ninth) of the total horses.
As it's impossible to divide 17 into half or 17 by 3
or 17 by 9, the three sons started to fight with each other.
So, they decided to go to a farmer friend who
they considered quite smart, to see if he

could work it out for them.

The farmer friend read the Will patiently, after giving due thought , he brought one of his own horses over and added it to the 17.

That increased the total to 18 horses.

Now, he divided the horses according to their father's will.

Half of 18 = 9. So he gave the eldest son 9 horses.

1/3rd of 18 = 6. So he gave the middle son 6 horses.

1/9th of 18 = 2. So he gave the youngest son 2 horses.

Now add up how many horses they have:

Eldest son 9

Middle son 6

Youngest son 2

TOTAL = 17

Now this leaves one horse over, so the farmer friend takes his horse back to his farm. Problem solved!

Moral: The attitude of negotiation and problem solving is to find the "18th horse", that is "the common ground".

Once a person is able to find the 18th horse, the issue is resolved.

It is difficult at times.

However, to reach a solution, the first step is to believe that there is a solution.

If we think that there is no solution, we won't be able to reach any!

That's what we call clever mathematics.

**

"Crime does not pay...as well as politics"
Ambrose Gwinnet (writer and wit)

**

A young woman was having her dreams analysed by a psychiatrist. One day she told him she hadn't dreamed the night before. "Young lady." He snapped "I cannot help you if you don't do your homework!"

<u>Shortest Speech Ever</u>

In a perfect world of multiculturism would mean exactly the following and people would move around understanding this simple rule.

No wonder Vladimir Putin was selected by Forbes as the most powerful person in the world. In this piece the Russian president, addressed the Duma, (Russian Parliament), and gave the following speech about the tensions with minorities in Russia:

"In Russia, live like Russians. Any minority, from anywhere, if it wants to live in Russia, to work and eat in Russia, it should speak Russian, and should respect the Russian laws. If they prefer Sharia Law, and live the life of Muslims, then we advise them to go to those places where that's the state law.

"Russia does not need Muslim minorities. Minorities need Russia, and we will not grant them special privileges, or try to change our laws to fit their desires, no matter how loud they yell 'discrimination'. We will not tolerate disrespect of our Russian culture.

The Muslims are taking over countries and they will not take over Russia. The Russian customs and traditions are not compatible with the lack of culture, or the primitive ways of Sharia Law and Muslims.

"When this honorable legislative body thinks of creating new laws, it should have in mind the Russian national interest first, observing that the Muslim Minorities are not Russians."

After the speech, the politicians in the Duma gave Putin a five-minute standing ovation!

**

<u>Variation Law</u> - *If you change lines (or traffic lanes), the first one will always move faster than the one you are in now.*
**

<u>Law of the Bath</u> - *When the body is fully immersed in water, the telephone will ring.*
**

A man filling in an application for duty in the U.S. Army Counter-Intelligence Corps found himself puzzling over the question 'Have you or any member of your relatives ever committed suicide?'

<u>*True Stories???*</u>
Well they could be!
Or they may have been made up!

1. AT&T fired President John Walter after nine months, saying he lacked intellectual leadership. He received a $26 million severance package.
Perhaps it's not Walter who's lacking intelligence.

2. WITH A LITTLE HELP FROM OUR FRIENDS: Police in Oakland, CA spent two hours attempting to subdue a gunman who had barricaded himself inside his home. After firing ten tear gas canisters, officers discovered that the man was standing beside them in the police line, shouting, ***'Please come out and give yourself up.'***

3. WHAT WAS PLAN B?
An Illinois man, pretending to have a gun, kidnapped a motorist and forced him to drive to two different automated teller machines, *wherein the kidnapper proceeded to withdraw money from his own bank accounts.*

4. THE GETAWAY!
A man walked into a Topeka, Kansas Kwik Stop and asked for all the money in the cash drawer. Apparently,

the take was too small, so he tied up the store clerk and *worked the counter himself for three hours until police showed up and grabbed him.*

5. DID I SAY THAT?

Police in Los Angeles had good luck with a robbery suspect who just couldn't control himself during a lineup. When detectives asked each man in the lineup to repeat the words: 'Give me all your money or I'll shoot', *the man shouted, 'that's not what I said!'*

6. THE GRAND FINALE!

Last summer, down on Lake Isabella, located in the high desert an hour east of Bakersfield, CA, some folks, new to boating, were having a problem. No matter how hard they tried, they couldn't get their brand new 22 foot boat, going. It was very sluggish in almost every manouvre, no matter how much power they applied. After about an hour of trying to make it go, they putted into a nearby marina, thinking someone there may be able to tell them what was wrong. A thorough topside check revealed everything in perfect working condition. The engine ran fine, the out-drive went up and down, and the propeller was the correct size and pitch. So, one of the marina guys jumped in the water to check underneath. *He came up choking on water, he was laughing so hard. Under the boat, still strapped securely in place, was the trailer!*

Friday's Bike Ride.

This could not have been Percy he does not ride a bike.

I went to the off-licence on Friday afternoon on my bicycle, bought a bottle of Red wine and put it in the bicycle basket.

As I was about to leave, I thought to myself that if I fell off the bicycle, the bottle would break. So I drank all the wine before I cycled home. It turned out to be a very good decision, because I fell off my bicycle seven times on the way home.

**

The Duck

A woman brought a very limp duck into a veterinary surgeon. As she laid her pet on the table, the vet pulled out his stethoscope and listened to the bird's chest. After a moment or two, the vet shook his head and sadly said, "I'm sorry, your duck, Cuddles, has passed away." The distressed woman wailed, "Are you sure?"

"Yes, I am sure. Your duck is dead," replied the vet. "How can you be so sure?" she protested.. "I mean you haven't done any testing on him or anything. He might just be in a coma or something."

The vet rolled his eyes, turned around and left the room. He returned a few minutes later with a black Labrador Retriever. As the duck's owner looked on in amazement, the dog stood on his hind legs, put his front paws on the examination table and sniffed the duck from top to bottom. He then looked up at the vet with sad eyes and shook his head. The vet patted the dog on the head and took it out of the room. A few minutes later he returned with a cat. The cat jumped on the table and also delicately sniffed the bird from head to foot. The cat sat back on its haunches, shook its head, meowed softly and strolled out of the room.

The vet looked at the woman and said, "I'm sorry, but as I said, this is most definitely, 100% certifiably, a "dead duck." The vet turned to his computer terminal, hit a few keys and produced a bill, which he handed to the woman.

The duck's owner, still in shock, took the bill. "$150!" she cried, "$150 just to tell me my duck is dead!"

The vet shrugged, "I'm sorry. If you had just taken my word for it, the bill would have been $20, but with the Lab Report and the Cat Scan, it's now $150.

Peas in a Pod
A lovely story all in rhyme...enjoy and totally true

"I have a curious tale to tell, of a life shared by two brothers.
The parents got on fairly well, but both were casual lovers.
The father was a reckless man who fought bravely in the war.
He met a younger woman, based on a friendly shore.
Coarse he was by nature, hers was tenderness with stress.
He often crudely teased her, but she liked him nonetheless.
Fondness turned to deep attraction, the future was held in dread.
It was a commonly held distraction that either could soon be dead.
The two hearts joined together, hoping for a lifetime bond,
Assuming love would last forever, not considering the beyond.
One year before war ended John, the first-born son, arrived.
It was what they both intended, and by luck they all survived.

In the final World-wide duel, the tide of battle turned.
The enemies, oh so cruel, reaped what they had earned.
Victory assured, peace was then declared.
Many wended their way home, to see how their families had fared.
Not much food lay on the tables,
The cupboards had been bared.

John had fondest memories of his early life.
There was food upon the table,
No signs of future strife.
Both parents had proven themselves able,

Story Telling Six

The husband and his wife.

It was quite a while before
There were any noticeable clashes.
Then the pair began their household war,
And mother suffered verbal lashes.

John himself could see, at an early age,
Sparring was restricted, in another sense:
When father had a sudden rage,
No blows did they exchange, nothing that intense!

The neighbours heard it all; John sat on the fence.
Trouble was a' brewing, he could clearly see.
Hopefully forgotten, he was not that dense.
Saying to himself,' it must not involve me!'

If Father lost a verbal spat
He laid the blame on John,
And said, 'The absence of a second brat
* Is down to you, I wish that you were gone!'*

But mother would have none of it, retorting viciously:
'The trouble lies with your magic wand, waved infrequently!
You must learn to use it more,
And thus extend the family!'

After years of enforced leisure
John was forced to go to school.
It was a statutory measure
So he obeyed the general rule.

Story Telling Six

Harsh discipline was widespread, considered as the norm.
It was applied by vicious teachers
Who would thrash him to conform.
They considered it their duty, to punish and inform.

In this establishment of learning
Where old-timers ruled the roost,
Some younger teachers more discerning
Arrived, and gave the place a welcome boost.

Their genteel style of teaching
Spared children from the rod,
Whilst the old ones gave a beating,
And thought the new approach most odd.

After ten long years of trying, father was a man relieved.
The day had come so had the man, seed sewn successfully!
The outcome had been timely, a second child conceived.
Mother's expectations met, she no longer felt aggrieved.

Yet, father asked himself: 'is mine a truly lucky state?
Am I not about to suffer the same uneasy fate?
As where a certain spider, eats her only mate?'
Of course there was no answer: he would have to wait.

As pregnancy progressed and mother's belly grew,
There existed in the love nest, mutual harmony.
A murmured cooing could be heard, twixt the feuding two.
Likewise John did benefit, as father let him be.

Then, inevitably it happened, to everyone's delight:
Thus a lusty baby howled its way into the light.

Story Telling Six

The home was full of jollity, happiness and joy.
Mother had given birth to Leon, a handsome baby boy!

Adults smiled with pleasure as baby opened his blue eyes,
Some chose to prod the little treasure, much to its surprise,
Then recoiled with disgust at the smell that did arise
As Leon broke wind noisily and bawled at his demise.

Mother calmly took the dirty diaper off the baby's bum,
And cleaned away the goo, before their startled eyes.
The howling was replaced with a gurgle and a hum.
But many felt a disgust that they could scarcely disguise

The more squeamish of the men, retreated to the back,
Many were complaining of feeling rather sick.
Women filled the empty spaces, taking up the slack,
Assessing the size of Leon's 'manhood', as only females could!

They considered it impressive in its potential size
As it lay there in its glory, all appeared to be fine.
Until the snake erected, spraying urine in their eyes.
The women pulled funny faces; it tasted not like sparkling wine!

All laughed with assumed jollity
At the nature of their demise,
Whilst Leon shared in their frivolity
But was really none the wise.

Just like his older brother,
Leon filled his infant years with fun.
The parents acted like new lovers
As if their married life had just begun.

Story Telling Six

The family changed their home, down a country lane to live.
In green fields the boys could roam, in a life of privilege.
A nearby school was found, it was indeed the Holy Grail:
No cruel teachers were around; new style teaching did prevail.
Father felt secure, his business a success.
Mother was less demure, he had caused her deep distress:
The house was his selection, he had fitted it throughout,
As a sign of his affection, he desired to leave her out
Of all the key decisions, for her to appreciate the more.
Ultimately, it would result in renewed household war.
It was intended as a blind gift, but had caused a major rift.
As the years flew by, in the twinkling of an eye,
John planned how best to flee this dismal nest.
Then realised he must wait, and accept his forlorn fate
Until he reached the age, where he could engage,
For a worthwhile wage, in a venture of his own.
When the time arrived (he surmised) his roots he could disown.
His father could be cruel, he was certainly most odd,
Yet how could John dislike him? They were two peas in the pod!
And so their lives continued, down a country lane.
John tried hard to study, but feared it was in vain.
He was also working early mornings and finding it a strain.
His father gave him no money, thought John was a drain
On family resources, said he would be happy when he finally left.
John tried hard not to show it, but felt inwardly bereft.
Mother was preoccupied, with mixed feelings of her own.
Leon was too young to understand, his wild seeds yet to be sewn.
John knew but a little of what young Leon did,
Except he loved all sport and was a healthy kid,
Swimming, rugby, cricket, Leon found them to be fun.

Story Telling Six

His English was not good, but you can't please everyone!

And so their lives continued, down a country lane.
The adults fought each other, with mutual disdain.
Leon's thoughts remained a mystery, his tongue he did constrain.
How it had come to this, no one could explain.

But look to the beginning, and remember this refrain:
When the two hearts joined together,
Hoping for a lifelong bond,
They assumed love would last forever,
And did not consider what went beyond.

Neither partner stopped to wonder
If they first should use their head.
That the marriage could split asunder
If they used their hearts instead.

Now mother stayed at home, doing things humdrum.
Father worked long hours, with little time for leisure.
Every night he snored, it was like a kettle drum,
Eating, reading, seeing TV, were their only forms of pleasure.

Mother was exhausted, to no one could she turn.
For separation from her husband, she began to yearn.
Soon to reach his early twenties, John had reached the age
Where limbo would be over, he could earn a decent wage.
He no longer had to wait, nor accept his current fate.
Lady luck had also chosen to take part in his life.
He met and fell in love with his gentle, pretty future wife.
John had used his head, not just his heart,

Story Telling Six

To help them both ensure that only death would see them part.
Soon church bells were a' ringing for John and his new wife.
Reflecting how his father had led a troubled life,
John vowed no wife of his, would undergo such strife.
The congregation sang as one, they were in finest voice.
In the marriage ceremony, they did heartily rejoice.

In the course of time, a sublime baby girl arrived.
The couple were delighted, they proudly spread the news.
John's mother shared their delight, the father felt deprived.
He quoted John this proverb, which bordered on abuse:
"Any fool is able to kick a hole in a tin can,
  But to add a spout to a kettle? It really takes a man!"

John's father remained oblivious to his mother's state of mind.
In matters of the heart, he was absolutely blind.
He paid her no attention, his neglect was most unkind.
She suffered from depression, until one day there came a man.
He was an enterprising farmer selling products from his van.
They both seduced each other, the father unaware.
She had fallen for the farmer, and no longer felt despair.
There they were each evening, hatching plans and making love,
Unaware of Leon, who heard all this, from his bed above.
He stayed awake all night, and piteously grieved:
His mother had betrayed him, he had been deceived.
But Leon was mistaken, his mother had been considerate.
She meant to take him with her, before it was too late.
Since father was not predictable in the matter of his fate.
The mother phoned John one day, her intentions to confide,
He already suspected this outcome, and so took her side.
As she planned to leave the gilded cage
Leon lay there miserably, whilst self-absorbed in rage.

Story Telling Six

It was just a few weeks later, when John picked up his phone.
The call was from his mother, he was worried by her tone.
Calmly she told him: "I have cancer of the breast,
It spread upwards from the womb." He did not hear the rest.
He spoke to his father, to see where matters stood,
Who said the end was near, and would do what he could.
The farmer, her intended, had a broken heart,
Whilst her husband observed his vow: "Till death us do part."
John and his family returned, down the country lane.
He and his wife hiding their sympathy and pain.
Their toddler hugged her Gran, who laughed her shared delight,
Though she was a sorry sight.

Leon's room was empty, he was nowhere to be found.
He had been told by father, to attend a camping ground
The father phoned one evening, finding it difficult to say,
'My wife has died in my arms, simply passed away.'
John drove his family back, down the country lane.
Mother had died young, his heart too was full of pain.
He stood outside his father's home, pondering what had passed.
"How sad it is!" He exclaimed, "They were reconciled at last!"
John to the parlour went, saw his mother in her coffin,
Had a final weep, kissed her brow, and gently tucked her in.
Leon showed no feelings, did he cry for the deceased?
No one knew nor could have guessed.

 Funeral traditions were upheld, the congregation in fine voice.
Hymns chosen were grief-stricken, no one wanted another choice.
Father stood at the front, with his sons in silent prayer.
Two of them at least, showed their despair.

Story Telling Six

The farmer stood at the back, in solitary grief.
Some in the congregation looked at him in disbelief.

And so this story ends, a sombre message for us all.
Act in haste, repent at leisure, expect choppy weather.
As regards Leon's inability, to ask and understand,
His father could be cruel, he was certainly most odd,
Yet both his sons were like him! They were three peas in a pod!
Copyright Terry Tumbler

**

"Be decisive. Right or wrong, make a decision. The road of life is paved with flat squirrels who couldn't make a decision."
~Unknown~

**

<u>**Law of Logical Argument**</u> -
Anything is possible IF you don't know what you are talking about.

Stuttering

A very pretty young speech therapist was getting nowhere with her stammerers Action group, an Englishman a Scotsman and an Irishman. She had tried every technique in the book without the slightest success.

Finally, thoroughly exasperated, she said "If any of you can tell me the name of the town where you were born, without stuttering, I will have wild and passionate sex with you until your muscles ache and your eyes water. So, who wants to go first?"

The Englishman piped up. "B-b-b-b-b-b-b-irmingham", he said. "That's no use, Trevor" said the speech therapist, "Who's next ?"

The Scotsman raised his hand and blurted out "P-p-p-p-p-p-p-p-p-aisley". That's no better. There'll be no sex for you, I'm afraid, Hamish. How about you, Paddy?

The Irishman took a deep breath and eventually blurted out "London ". Brilliant, Paddy! said the speech therapist and immediately set about living up to her promise.

After 15 minutes of exceptionally steamy sex, the couple paused for breath and Paddy said "-d-d-d-d-d-d-d-d-erry".

US Marine John Kelly was the last person to be awarded 2 Medals of Honor. He ran 100 yards in advance of the front line and attacked an enemy machine gun nest, killed the gunner with a grenade, shot another man with his pistol, and returned with 8 prisoners. He was 19.

**

Life can be accepted or changed. If it is not accepted then it must be changed. If it cannot be changed, then it must be accepted.
Sir Winston Churchill

Lovely Children?

1) NUDITY
I was driving with my three young children one warm summer evening when a woman in the convertible ahead of us stood up and waved. She was stark naked! As I was reeling from the shock, I heard my 5-year-old shout from the back seat, 'Mum, that lady isn't wearing a seat belt!'

2) OPINIONS
On the first day of school, a first-grader handed his teacher a note from his mother. The note read, 'The opinions expressed by this child are not necessarily those of his parents.'

3) TOMATO SAUCE
A woman was trying hard to get the tomato sauce out of the bottle. During her struggle the phone rang so she asked her 4-year-old daughter to answer the phone. 'Mummy can't come to the phone to talk to you right now. She's hitting the bottle.'

4) MORE NUDITY
A little boy got lost at the YMCA and found himself in the women's locker room. When he was spotted, the room burst into shrieks, with ladies grabbing towels and running for cover. The little boy watched in amazement and then asked, 'What's the matter, haven't you ever seen a little boy before?'

5) POLICE # 1

While taking a routine vandalism report at a primary school, I was interrupted by a little girl about 6 years old. Looking up and down at my uniform, she asked, 'Are you a policewoman? Yes,' I answered and continued writing the report. My mother said if I ever needed help I should ask the police. Is that right?' 'Yes, that's right,' I told her. 'Well, then,' she said as she extended her foot toward me, 'would you please tie my shoe lace?'

6) POLICE # 2

It was the end of the day when I parked my police van in front of the station. As I gathered my equipment, my police dog, Jake, was barking, and I saw a little boy staring in at me. 'Is that a dog you got back there?' he asked.

'It sure is,' I replied.

Puzzled, the boy looked at me and then towards the back of the van. Finally he said, 'What'd he do?'

7) ELDERLY

While working for meals on wheels delivering lunches to the elderly, I used to take my 4-year-old daughter on my rounds. She was unfailingly intrigued by the various appliances of old age, particularly the canes, walkers and wheelchairs. One day I found her staring at a pair of false teeth soaking in a glass. As I braced myself for the inevitable barrage of questions, she merely turned and whispered, 'The tooth fairy will never believe this!'

8) DRESS-UP

A little girl was watching her parents dress for a party. When she saw her dad donning his dinner suit, she warned, 'Daddy, you shouldn't wear that suit.'
'And why not, darling?'
'You know that it always gives you a headache the next morning.'

9) DEATH

While walking along the footpath in front of his church, our minister heard the intoning of a prayer that nearly made his collar wilt. Apparently, his 5-year-old son and his playmates had found a dead robin. Feeling that a proper burial should be performed, they had secured a small box and cotton wadding, then dug a hole and made ready for the disposal of the deceased. The minister's son was chosen to say the appropriate prayers and with sonorous dignity intoned his version of what he thought his father always said: 'Glory be unto the Faaather, and unto the Sonnn, and into the hole he goooes.'

10) SCHOOL

A little girl had just finished her first week of school. 'I'm just wasting my time,' she said to her mother. 'I can't read, I can't write, and they won't let me talk!'

Chinese Baby

Su Wong marries Lee Wong. The next year, the Wongs have a new baby. The nurse brings out a lovely, healthy, bouncy, but definitely a Caucasian, WHITE baby boy.

'Congratulations,' says the nurse to the new parents. 'Well Mr. Wong, what will you and Mrs. Wong name the baby?'

The puzzled father looks at his new baby boy and says, 'Well, two Wong's don't make a white, so I think we will name him...Sum Ting Wong

**

A publics works labourer was filling in a job questionnaire. To the question "Who is your immediate supervisor?" he wrote "My wife!"

**

A Dublin girl leaving the theatre with her companion after a performance of 'Les Miserables' asked "It was nice but who was Les?"

Any drugs, alcohol?

No thanks, I've got everything.

The Persian
Dancer (1915-1935)

Dancing was the young woman's all-consuming passion
in life. Since she had been a little girl, Kate had lived to
seize any opportunity to put on a party dress and dance to
any kind of music, even if it was only to the jaunty tunes
in her head. She played her parents' radio and all the
records in their limited collection endlessly, urging them
to buy more. She would jump for joy whenever there
was a Friday afternoon country dancing session at her
primary school. Without hesitation, she would drag the
nearest shy and blushing boy into her arms without a
trace of self consciousness.

Kate was a very popular girl, regularly attending friends'
parties, but she was far less interested in going out to play

with anyone than in daydreaming at home alone. She
much preferred spending time in her own fantasy world.
She would love nothing better than to dress her beloved
tabby cat Mickey in one of her homemade tutus, if he
would stay still long enough. He had quickly cottoned on
to this ritual humiliation and tried to make a dash for the
bottom of the garden whenever he saw the beaming girl
approaching, armed with a costume. She practiced her
best dance moves with poor, bemused Mickey, to a
musical accompaniment, and usually during a prolonged
bout of joyful giggling.

Mickey generally slept in Kate's room, either curled up at
the end of the bed or nuzzling against her under the
covers, and he featured in most of her favourite dreams:
Sometimes the two of them would be running a Dance
Academy, giving demonstrations of their routines. At
other times they would be involved in a Hollywood
musical, dancing alongside Kate's favourite stars.
However, her favourite scenario involved them dancing
together on stage during a sold-out tour, she in an elegant
dress and Mickey looking dapper in top hat and tails.
They always received rapturous applause from an
enthralled audience which comprised of adults, children
and a variety of small animals and cartoon characters.

She begged her parents to let her have ballet lessons,
offering to forgo all her pocket money for the duration of
her childhood. She also asked for dancing shoes for
several birthdays. Kate quickly progressed to taking part
in local competitions, which she often won. Her family
and friends would come to watch her, and she relished

performing in front of any kind of audience, playing to the gallery on every occasion. Kate's motivation was so strong and the adrenaline rush so exhilarating. She drove herself to practice for several hours every day, reading all the dancing books she could find and doing anything she could to improve her skills and increase her experience, ignoring the aches and pains that came along with her success.

Kate was an only child, and her wealthy lawyer parents were keen to help and support her towards achieving her dreams, but they also wanted to ensure that she appreciated the value of money and did not become spoilt. However, they were delighted to see that she was growing up to be a delightful, sensible, caring and considerate young woman. When she enrolled in a course of Performing Arts at the local College, they decided to splash out on a second-hand car to give her a taste of independence. She was, of course, elated about this incredibly generous gift. Not only did she use her car every day, but she was also happy to give lifts to her friends.

She loved the course, especially the practical elements. During the first year she developed a keen interest in ballroom dancing. She embraced its timeless elegance and grace, and worked very hard to master the techniques to perfection. She lived for losing herself in each movement and vibrant moment on the dance floor. It was at a special evening of ballroom dancing that one of the young men asked her out on a date. She had danced with him many times, liked him very much, and felt a thrill of embarrassed excitement at having been asked. However, she had mixed feelings and had told him she would think about it and let him know the next day.

As she drove home that evening, Kate was barely aware of the high winds and heavy rain buffeting the car because her mind was spinning with fevered excitement and anticipation. She knew she was becoming very accomplished at ballroom dancing, and wondered if it would be possible to master other styles and ultimately be able to pursue a career in an activity that she loved so much. She had just started to question herself about whether she wanted to risk diluting the pure joy of dancing with the distraction of a relationship, and possibly jeopardise a pleasant friendship, when a cat suddenly appeared from nowhere out of the darkness into her headlights just as she was approaching a very sharp bend.

Kate had been driving down the familiar country lane a bit too quickly in the rapidly deteriorating weather conditions, and had no time to think. Her desperate attempt at an emergency stop led to the car skidding off the wet road and into a sickening head-on collision with a tree. Kate was killed instantly. A Persian cat, totally unscathed, stood looking at the mangled wreckage for a few moments, watching the wisps of smoke disperse and the back wheels until they stopped turning. She rippled her fur against the raindrops which were falling on her body, and then ambled back into the wood from which she had just emerged.

Cat Lady (1935 - 2015)

The elderly lady had always been more than happy living alone. During her long life, Katherine had made many friends and saw them from time to time, but only when it suited her, and strictly on her terms. She tended to lose touch with people when they moved away, and she reserved the right to cancel any arrangements at the last moment if she felt like it. While she was generally quite friendly, and could be loving when she chose to be, she had a tendency to turn cool towards people on a whim. She was content about having a reputation for being somewhat enigmatic, sometimes aloof, and always fiercely independent.

She had shared the majority of her life with a series of cats. Every one of them had been so precious, such unique and unforgettable characters. She felt that she had never fully recovered from the trauma of losing her first cat, a grey tabby called Emma, to an evil hit-and-run motorist when she was only five. It had taken nearly two years before she could even consider having another fur baby in her life. Jezebel, a tortoiseshell beauty with a permanently damp nose and tiny ears, had seen her through her teenage years, listening without judgement even during her final illness. How could she ever forget mottled Mr Mistopheles, whose timeless wisdom had been reflected in his every gesture and expression for over twenty years? Every one of them was irreplaceable, and without exception she preferred them to people.

The only annual social event that Katherine made a point of attending was a Halloween party held by her neighbour. Never caring what clothes other people might be wearing, she would don a different cat costume on each occasion. She would spend many months creating her outfit, lingering lovingly over the sewing and finer points of embroidery, taking her time to ensure the design and colour of each paw was just right. The tail needed to be crafted properly, each whisker straightened and configured, while the shape and size of such key features as her nose and ears could not be overlooked. Every year she would slink around the room in her cat guise for a while, selecting a few items from the buffet to put into the special bowl that she always brought with her; she did not mingle as such or speak to other guests, preferring to retreat to watch proceedings from the safe distance of the comfiest looking sofa. She would never announce her departure, slipping away silently as soon as she started to feel bored or could think of a better place to be.

On her final night Katherine dozed off a couple of times while watching TV, feeling more weary than usual. She managed to muster enough strength to take herself to bed early, but she slept lightly and awoke with a start around midnight. Looking around the room, she could not see anything out of the ordinary, but sensed that something was amiss and she now felt wide awake and fully alert. She fancied having a snack before trying to go back to sleep, so decided to go downstairs to get something for herself and also see if her feline friends might be interested in some water and a few biscuits themselves.

Upon entering the living room, the lady stopped for a moment to inspect the room. She wrinkled her nose, rubbed her eyes gently then opened them wide in the darkness. She had become accustomed to being able to see quite clearly at night without needing to turn on the light or even put on her glasses. The striking black and white light and shadows reminded her of an atmospheric film noir from the 1940s. While there were no famous Hollywood actors in this particular scene, her cats were always the main characters, her protagonists. They were all looking at her, blinking softly and kneading various items of the furniture in rapt anticipation.

The woman started padding towards the kitchen, but after just a few steps she was suddenly struck by debilitating shooting pains. She pulled up, rooted to the spot in shock, gasping, then helplessly clutching her chest, before slumping heavily back onto the settee. Breathing fitfully now and finding her nightdress had quickly become drenched in a profuse sweat which was running alternately fiery hot then as cold as stone. Katherine could feel her consciousness starting to slip away, her senses fading; Her faltering hands reached out to touch and stroke her beloved cats, giving her the familiar warmth of joy, inner peace and relief.

Veteran campaigner Ginger's drilling slowly started up, like a well-oiled motor running smoothly on a sub-zero winter's morning, an engine so efficient and never likely to stall. As ever, his little sister Lily languidly cleaned her pristine white fur and would stretch all her limbs and twitch her tail several times before deigning to purr. Little black kitten Thomas flexed his tiny claws, then dribbled happily, accepting the lady's affection while lying on his back; then a moment later he was beady-eyed, pupils dilating, standing bolt upright, on sentry duty; in another instant he was gone, heading for the shadows behind the curtains, without looking back.

The next day, her neighbour, who was concerned that Katherine had given her apologies for the previous night's Halloween party, decided to check on her and bring her a piece of cake. As she entered the house she was shocked to find that the poor old woman had passed away. The neighbour had known Katherine for a long time, but she had never felt very close to her, and she had no idea about who the next of kin might be. She was familiar with the three cats in the living room, they looked content and very well as ever. They were lounging around on the armchairs, focused on the task of grooming themselves thoroughly.

However, the neighbour was surprised to see a fourth cat in the room, a sleek Persian with striking, sharp blue eyes. She was standing a short distance away from the others, next to the television, which was showing an old film featuring Fred Astaire and Ginger Rogers dancing cheek-to-cheek. The cat looked away from the black-and-white images just for a moment, to give the intruder a marked look of indifference, before returning her gaze to the screen. **Copyright Richard Seal 2017**

<u>*A Love Story*</u>

I will seek and find you.
I shall take you to bed, and have my way with you.
I will make you ache, shake & sweat until you moan
& groan.
I will make you beg for mercy, beg for me to stop.
I will exhaust you to the point that you will be
relieved when I'm finished with you.
And, when I am finished, you will be weak for days.
All my love, Signed: The Flu...**If it is the right time
of the year flu shot!**

**

**Law of Commercial Marketing Strategy -
As soon as you find a product that you
really like, they will stop making it OR the
store will stop selling it!**

**

*Reporters interviewing a 104-year-old
woman: 'And what do you think is the best
thing about being 104?' the reporter
asked... She simply replied, 'No peer
pressure.'*

Never Forget

James often had a little smile to himself, bemused about the fact that he had lived such a long life. He seemed to have escaped unscathed from the effects of smoking cigarettes throughout most of his adult life; he had always enjoyed drinking, and had never been a big fan of eating healthily either. His idea of exercise had seldom extended far beyond a half-hearted jog to the pub when last orders was getting a bit too close for comfort ...

Sensing the anticipation starting to build around him, James glanced at his watch and was not surprised to see that the old year now had only a few minutes remaining. He drained his pint with relish and finished his last sausage roll. While the family and friends gathered around were all younger than him, he always felt happy and comfortable in their company. He was enveloped by a familiar beery warmth as he was helped to his feet.

As he linked arms with his lovely nieces, James wondered how many times he had heard 'Auld Lang Syne' on New Year's Eve. It seemed to have a deeper resonance since his beloved wife Ellen had passed, of course .. Stepping forward he could sense her beside him, her thigh pressed against his as always, her rich voice singing with passion deep within, while his mother's hand continued to squeeze joy from his heart as the chorus reached a crescendo.

As the ring broke, James felt his Dad's arms holding him

safely, keeping him steady on his first bike ... The song continued to echo throughout his being, heightening his senses as the New Year chimes heralded hugs and kisses from loved ones in the old man's past and present. Through the laughter and tears, old acquaintances never to be forgotten.

Copyright Richard Seal 2017

**

Man at a restaurant table to a waiter – "What's my offence? I have been on bread and water for two hours."

**

Tenants Complaints!

Extracts from letters written by tenants:

1. It's the dog's mess that I find hard to swallow.
2. I want some repairs done to my cooker as it has backfired and burnt my knob off.
3. I wish to complain that my father twisted his ankle very badly when he put his foot in the hole in his back passage.
4. Their 18 year old son is continually banging his balls against my fence.
5. I wish to report that tiles are missing from the outside toilet roof. I think it was bad wind the other day that blew them off.
6. My lavatory seat is cracked, where do I stand?
7. Will you please send someone to mend the garden

path. My wife tripped and fell on it yesterday and now she is pregnant.

8. I request permission to remove my drawers in the kitchen.

9. I am writing on behalf of my sink, which is coming away from the wall.

10. 50% of the walls are damp, 50% have crumbling plaster, and 50% are just plain filthy.

11. The next door neighbour has got this huge tool that vibrates the whole house and I just can't take it anymore.

12. The toilet is blocked and we cannot bath the children until it is cleared.

13. Will you please send a man to look at my water, it is a funny colour and not fit to drink.

14. Our lavatory seat is broken in half and now is in three pieces.

15. I want to complain about the farmer across the road. Every morning at 6am his cock wakes me up and it's now getting too much for me.

16. The man next door has a large erection in the back garden, which is unsightly and dangerous.

17. Our kitchen floor is damp. We have two children and would like a third, so please send someone round to do something about it.

18. I am a single woman living in a downstairs flat and would you please do something about the noise made by the man on top of me every night.

19. Please send a man with the right tool to finish the job and satisfy my wife.   **

Story Telling Six

Let's Talk Brexit

Mr Dave Davis is at the golf club returning his locker key when Mr Barnier, the membership secretary sees him.

"Hello Mr Davis", says Mr Barnier. "I'm sorry to hear you are no longer renewing your club membership, if you would like to come to my office we can settle your account".

"I have settled my bar bill" says Mr Davis. "Ah yes Mr Davis", says Mr Barnier, "but there are other matters that need settlement" In Mr Barnier's office - Mr Davis explains that he has settled his bar bill so wonders what else he can possibly owe the Golf Club?

"Well Mr Davis" begins Mr Barnier, "you did agree to buy one of our Club Jackets". "Yes" agrees Mr Davis "I did agree to buy a jacket, but I haven't received it yet. As soon as you supply the jacket I will send you a cheque for the full amount".

"That will not be possible" explains Mr Barnier. "As you are no longer a club member you will not be entitled to buy one of our jackets"!

"But you still want me to pay for it" exclaims Mr Davis. "Yes" says Mr Barnier, "That will be £500 for the jacket. "There is also your bar bill".

Story Telling Six

"But I've already settled my bar bill" says Mr Davis. "Yes" says Mr Barnier, "but as you can appreciate, we need to place our orders from the Brewery in advance to ensure our bar is properly stocked. You regularly used to spend at least £50 a week in the bar so we have placed orders with the brewery accordingly for the coming year.. You therefore owe us £2600 for the year".

"Will you still allow me to have these drinks?" asks Mr Davis. "No of course not Mr Davis". "You are no longer a club member!" says Mr Barnier. "Next is your restaurant bill" continues Mr Barnier. "In the same manner we have to make arrangements in advance with our catering suppliers. Your average restaurant bill was in the order of £300 a month, so we'll require payment of £3600 for the next year".

"I don't suppose you'll be letting me have these meals either" asks Mr Davis. "No, of course not" says an irritated Mr Barnier, "you are no longer a club member! Then of course" Mr Barnier continues, "there are repairs to the clubhouse roof".

"Clubhouse roof" exclaims Mr Davis, "What's that got to do with me?" "Well it still needs to be repaired and the builders are coming in next week", your share of the bill is £2000". "I see" says Mr Davis, "anything else?".

"Now you mention it" says Mr Barnier, "there is Fred the Barman's pension. We would like you to pay £5 a week towards Fred's pension when he retires next month. He's not well you know so I doubt we'll need to ask you for payment for longer than about five years, so £1300 should do it. This brings your total bill to £10,000" says Mr Barnier.

"Let me get this straight" says Mr Davis, "you want me to pay £500 for a jacket you won't let me have, £2600 for beverages you won't let me drink and £3600 for food you won't let me eat, all under a roof I won't be allowed under and not served by a bloke who's going to retire next month!"

"Yes, it's all perfectly clear and quite reasonable" says Mr Barnier. "P*ss off!" says Mr Davis and walks out. **Now we understand what Brexit is all about!!!!!**
**

Fishy!

All throughout dinner my wife's best friend's four-year-old daughter stared at me as I sat opposite her.
The girl could hardly eat her food for staring. I checked my shirt for spots, felt my face for food, and patted my hair in place, but nothing stopped her from staring at me.

Finally I asked her, *"Why are you staring at me?"*
Everyone at the table had noticed her behavior, and the table went quiet, waiting for her response.

The little girl said, *"I'm just waiting to see how you drink like a fish."*

The Football Fan

Primary Teacher explains to her class that she is a Liverpool fan. She asks her students to raise their hands if they too are Liverpool fans.

Everyone in the class raises their hand except one little girl.

The teacher looks at the girl with surprise and says,

'Mary, why didn't you raise your hand?'

'Because I'm not a Liverpool fan,' she replied.

The teacher, still shocked, asked, 'Well, if you are not a Liverpool fan, then who are you a fan of?'

'I am a Chelsea fan, and proud of it,' Mary replied.

The teacher could not believe her ears. 'Mary, why, pray tell, are you a Chelsea fan?'

'Because my mum is a Chelsea fan, and my dad is a Chelsea fan, so I'm a Chelsea fan too!'

'Well,' said the teacher in an obviously annoyed tone, 'that is no reason for you to be a Chelsea fan. You don't have to be just like your parents all of the time... What if your mum was a prostitute and your dad was a drug addict, what would you be then?'

'Then' Mary smiled, 'I'd be a Liverpool fan.

The Job

A man walked into the local job centre, marched straight up to the Counter and said 'Hi, I'm looking for a job'.

The man behind the counter replied 'Your timing is amazing'. We've just got one in from a very wealthy man who wants a chauffeur/bodyguard for his nymphomaniac twin daughters. You'll have to drive around in a big black Mercedes and wear the uniform provided. The hours are a bit long but the meals are also provided. You also have to escort the young ladies on their overseas holidays. The Salary package is £200,000 a year'.

The Scouser said 'You're bullshitting me!'

The man behind the counter said 'Well you started it!'

**

Police in Liverpool last night announced the discovery of an arms cache of 200 semi-automatic rifles with 25,000 rounds of ammunition, 20 tons of heroin, £5 million in forged UK banknotes and 25 trafficked Ukrainian prostitutes, all in a semi-detached house> behind the Public Library in Toxteth. Local residents were stunned, and a community spokesman said:"We're all really shocked; we never knew we had a library."

**

<u>Missing</u>

Anthony had been so happy to travel by train down to Essex to visit his best friend Chris, who had moved away from the Midlands two years previously on promotion to Head of History at a Girls' Grammar School. After meeting as teenagers when they worked at their local pub, they had enjoyed going out for a few pints every Friday night for many years afterwards. Originally there had been five of them in their pub-crawling group, but Chris and Anthony had always got on particularly well with each other and gradually the others had moved away. Anthony had never liked any of them very much anyway, they all seemed more knowing, somehow less genuine, so he was pleased when it was just the two of them. He had really missed his friend since he had headed south - the occasional message or phone call was not the same as having a few laughs with a lot of beers.

It had been a particularly hectic week at work, but Anthony was really looking forward to catching up with Chris over a long weekend, staying at his flat, and sampling the local ales. Arriving at Southend station earlier than expected, Anthony had retired to a bench to wait for his friend. He had felt very tired, and was glad to have the chance to relax and re-energize for a while. Then again, when Chris arrived their reunion felt curiously flat. Anthony had the unsettling feeling that Chris was not quite himself, he seemed quiet, distracted and somewhat distant. However, Anthony reflected that it had been quite a while since their last meeting and he put the awkwardness down to nerves or a little shyness - a pub crawl seemed the ideal way to break the ice, of course, and he had felt sure that they would soon be having lots of fun together again, just like in the good old days.

After dropping his bag off at the flat, Chris took Anthony straight out for a few drinks in the old part of Leigh-on-Sea. The town was really busy on that warm Friday evening in late September. As they were standing up at the bar in the third pub, and the alcohol was just starting to have the desired effect, Anthony suddenly became aware of a group of men talking to each other just behind them, and spotted one of them pointing at Chris. Anthony nudged his friend, and felt a shiver run down his spine as the men approached. They ignored Anthony and spoke to Chris:

"Hey Mike, mate, what are you doing here?", the tallest man in the group spoke with doubt, possibly a little confusion in his voice.

"Yeah, man, we didn't expect to see you here!" said the second man. "What are you up to?"

Chris turned slowly to look at the group, gave them a half-smile and spoke slowly. "I'm sorry, guys, I'm not Mike. My name's Chris."

"Come off it, Mike, stop mucking around. Why are you here?" said the third man, who sounded more threatening than jocular.

"Honestly, you're making a mistake." Chris paused, seeming

lost in thought for a moment. "I'm a teacher, I live here now, but originally come from Birmingham."

The men looked at each other in silence, before fixing their glares on Chris. "You're the one who's made a mistake. I don't know what you're playing at, mate, you know who you are!"

Chris's smile faded away. "Look, I'm not ... "

The first man stepped forward, grasped the lapel of Chris's jacket and hissed "Look - you are Mike, don't try denying it again! Do you think we're stupid?"

Chris turned very pale suddenly. He put his face in his hands for what seemed like a couple of minutes, shaking his head a couple of times. Eventually he looked up, turned to Anthony for a moment with a haunted expression and a blank, hollow look in his eyes, then he looked at the three men, attempting another thin smile.

"OK, you got me, guys, I'm bang to rights. What can I say?" His voice sounded different somehow.

"Plenty. You've got a lot of explaining to do, where have you been ... "

The other two men had just started moving closer when Chris suddenly slipped away and bolted straight out of a side door. In an instant he had disappeared, with the second and third men following in hot pursuit, knocking a couple of chairs over in the process. Many pairs of eyes were now trained on Anthony and the remaining man, and a couple of people looked as if they were considering coming over to them before thinking better of it. Anthony looked at the man, who was silently contemplating his pint, and plucked up the courage to speak.

"What is going on here? I have known Chris for years, he is not your friend. They must just look like each other I guess."

It was like the man had not even heard Anthony speak. He did not reply, or even look up from his glass. He finished his drink, then walked out. Anthony felt very confused and increasingly anxious as he left the pub. He was not sure what to think about the bizarre events unfolding around him. He tried ringing Chris, but was shocked to hear a message informing him that the number was not recognised. Should he go and start looking for him? Anthony did not know the town and was not even sure that he could remember the way back to the flat. As long as he could find his way there, he supposed he could wait there until Chris got home.

It appear to take Anthony hours to find the narrow street, lined with Victorian terraces, which all seemed to look the same in the dark; several people who he tried to ask for directions did not stop, they just continued walking. By the time he reached the place he felt stone-cold sober, chilly and tired, but his senses were sharply awakened by the sight of the boarded-up building in front of him. It did not look like the place had been lived in for some time, there were no signs of life at all. Rooted to the spot, he stared at it with a growing sense of disbelief and fear. Panicking now, Anthony tried ringing home and other friends, but found that none of the numbers were in use. Who were the men in the pub? What had happened to his bag with all his things?

At a complete loss at what to do, Anthony went into a nearby twenty four hour cafe to try to calm himself down, but no one acknowledged his presence and the waitress ignored his request for a coffee. He sat in a booth in the corner, feeling dazed, eventually managing to doze a little until it started to get light. His head ached and his mouth felt very dry as he left the cafe on the sunny Saturday morning. There was a small park nearby, into which Anthony found himself wandering aimlessly. He was struggling to get his bleary thoughts into some kind of order when he saw a familiar figure sitting on a bench, reading a newspaper. He rubbed his face, and blinked hard a couple of times before crying out Chris's name and running to greet him. However, he was shocked to receive absolutely no reaction. Anthony seized Chris's shoulder and found it hard to resist the temptation to shake him hard.

"For God's sake, Chris, where have you been? What on Earth is going on? Is this some kind of a joke?"

As he stared into his friend's eyes he thought he saw a very brief glimmer of recognition, but Chris said nothing and looked beyond him as if there were no-one there. Overcome with a deep sense of foreboding, Anthony took his hand away and watched Chris put on a pair of sunglasses, stand up and walk slowly away. Anthony froze, unable to do anything other than watch him leave.

He looked down at the paper that Chris had left on the bench. He was puzzled to see that the date at the top of the page was over a year and a half ago. Then the headline caught his eye: 'Disappearance of popular Southend teacher'. Anthony was halted in his tracks when he realised that the article was about his friend. Struggling to breathe with his heart thundering at an alarming rate, he was filled with further terror when he continued reading: "Reynolds was last seen at Southend station. Police want to speak to local man Mike Harris, in connection with his disappearance." The picture of Reynolds looked like Chris.

After pulling himself together, Anthony rallied and ran in the direction that he had seen Chris heading. He caught up with him, but instead of endeavouring to speak to him this time he hung back and followed him at a discreet distance. After about twenty minutes they arrived at the railway station. There were a lot of people around that morning and Anthony found it difficult to keep an eye on Chris through the melee. The tension increased further as the man kept biting his nails, looking anxiously at his watch, then glanced over his shoulder several times.

Just after an announcement that an express train was passing through the station, events seemed to go in slow motion. Anthony lost sight of Chris just before the train came to a shrieking halt, and a momentary silence was shattered by a series of shouts and screams. A crowd of people gathered very quickly, looking down at the tracks. He could not get close enough to see what had happened, but he did spot the three men from the pub as they broke free from the group and walked past him. He thought he saw a hint of a smile on one of the faces, looking at him briefly, as the men strolled towards the escalators ... Anthony could feel himself starting to lose consciousness, and managed to make it to a nearby seat before everything went black ...

A familiar voice caused Anthony to open his eyes and look up slowly. "Wake up, buddy. I hope you enjoyed your forty winks! I'm sorry I'm late, I hope you haven't been waiting here too long." The man's smile slipped to a frown for a moment. "What's up? Who's been walking on your grave?"

Anthony looked at his friend's cheerful face, the throbbing in his head starting to ease a little. "Chris?" The platform was busy, with a lot of people coming and going, but there was no sign of the crowd or the express train. Nothing looked out of the ordinary.

"Who were you expecting?" Chris laughed and patted him on the back. "I hope the journey down was okay. Come on, bring your bag. I'll take you to the flat, then we'll head into town for a few beers ... "

Anthony pulled the newspaper out of his jacket pocket and found it was that day's edition. He was mightily relieved to see no sign of the story about a missing teacher. Chris watched him with a bemused expression. Anthony stumbled over his words, which seemed to be stuck in his throat ... "But what about ... "

" ... Food? Trust you! Don't worry about that, I'm sure we can get a bag of crisps or nuts in one of the pubs. Perhaps a kebab or curry later, if you like!" Chris put his arm round Anthony's shoulder. "There are several pints with our names out there tonight, my friend, and we don't want to keep them waiting, do we?"

They left the station together laughing and looking forward to an enjoyable reunion weekend. Neither of them noticed the three men who were sitting together at the station bar watching the two friends walk out ...

Copyright Richard Seal 2017

**

"I am enclosing two tickets to the first night of my new play; bring a friend, if you have one." -George Bernard Shaw to Winston Churchill "Cannot possibly attend first night, will attend second... if there is one." -Winston Churchill, in response

**

The Bar

Spare a thought for poor ole Michael O'Leary, Chief Executive of Ryanair.

After arriving in a hotel in Manchester, he went to the bar and asked for a pint of Guinness. The barman nodded and said, "That will be £1 please, Mr O'Leary."

Somewhat taken aback, O'Leary replied, "That's very cheap," and handed over his money.

"Well, we do try to stay ahead of the competition", said the barman. "And we are serving free pints every Wednesday from 6 pm until 8 pm. We have the cheapest beer in England".

"That is remarkable value", Michael comments.

"I see you don't seem to have a glass, so you'll probably need one of ours. That will be £3 please."

O'Leary scowled, but paid up..

He took his drink and walked towards a seat. "Ah, you want to sit down?" said the barman. "That'll be an extra £2. You could have pre-booked the seat, and it would have only cost you £1.

"I think you may be too big for the seat sir, can I ask you to sit in this frame please". Michael attempts to sit down but the frame is too small and when he can't squeeze in, he complains "Nobody would fit in that little frame".

"I'm afraid if you can't fit in the frame you'll have to pay an extra surcharge of £4 for your seat sir".

Leary swore to himself, but paid up. "I see that you have brought your laptop with you" added the barman. "And since that wasn't pre-booked either, that will be another £3."

O'Leary was so incensed that he walked back to the bar, slammed his drink on the counter, and yelled, "This is ridiculous, I want to speak to the manager".

"I see you want to use the counter," says the barman, "that will be £2 please."

O'Leary's face was red with rage. "Do you know who I am?" "Of course I do Mr O'Leary."

"I've had enough! What sort of a Hotel is this? I come in for a quiet drink and you treat me like this. I insist on speaking to a manager!"

"Here is his e-mail address, or if you wish, you can contact him between 9.00 am and 9.01am every morning, Monday to Tuesday at this free phone number. Calls are free, until they are answered, then there is a talking charge of only £1 per second, or part thereof".

"I will never use this bar again".

"OK sir, but do remember, we are the only hotel in England selling pints for £1."

**

The positive thinker sees the invisible, feels the intangible and achieves the impossible.

Sir Winston Churchill

Unbeatable

A seven year old boy was at the centre of a courtroom drama where he challenged a court ruling over who should have custody of him. The boy has a history of being beaten by his parents and the judge initially awarded custody to his aunt, in keeping with the child custody law and regulations requiring that family unity be maintained to the degree possible.

The boy surprised the court when he proclaimed that his aunt beat him more than his parents and he adamantly refused to live with her. When the judge suggested that he live with his grandparents, the boy cried out that they also beat him.

After considering the remainder of the immediate family and learning that domestic violence was apparently a way of life among them, the judge took the unprecedented step of allowing the boy to propose who should have custody of him.

After two recesses to check legal references and confer with child welfare officials, the judge granted temporary custody to the England Cricket team, which the boy firmly believes is not capable of beating anyone.

Quiet Golf.

We don't know if this is true, but it is funny.

It was back in the 70's and a soon-to-be prominent and rather arrogant (Ray Floyd) was playing at Augusta in his first Masters.

Back then the players could not bring their own caddies. They had to use one of the locals.
Floyd told the Caddy Master he wanted a big fellow who could handle his bag, but who also would keep quiet, no advice needed.
The caddy who was assigned Floyd said, "Hello Mr. Floyd."
Floyd said "Hello." And followed with: "That's the last I want to hear from you unless I ask you a question."
Everything went well until the 10th hole when Floyd pushed his drive into the right trees on the par 4. After surveying the scene, he said out loud, "I'm going to hit a low fade out through that opening to carry and land mid

green and then roll over the crest down near the hole."
Surprisingly he pulled it off exactly and turned to his caddy and said, "How's that?"
The caddy spoke for the first time and said, "That wasn't your ball."
**

<u>MEDICARE</u>

If you are an older senior citizen and can no longer take care of yourself and need Long-Term Care, but the government says there is no Nursing Home care available for you, what do you do?

You may opt for Medicare Part G.
The plan gives anyone 75 or older a gun (Part G) and one bullet. You may then shoot one worthless politician. This means you will be sent to prison for the rest of your life where you will receive three meals a day, a roof over your head, central heating and air conditioning, cable TV, a library, and all the health care you need.

Need new teeth? No problem.
Need glasses? That's great.

Need a hearing aid, new hip, knees, kidney, lungs, sex change, or heart?
They are all covered!
As an added bonus, your kids can come and visit you at least as often as they do now! And, who will be paying for all of this? The same government that just told you they can't afford for you to go into a nursing home.
And you will get rid of a useless politician while you are at it. And now, because you are a prisoner, you don't have to pay any more income taxes!

**

"He has Van Gogh's ear for music." - Billy Wilder

**

"Some cause happiness wherever they go; others, whenever they go." - Oscar Wilde

**

"I didn't attend the funeral, but I sent a nice letter saying I approved of it." - Mark Twain

Headlong

Jenny has always insisted that her young family makes an annual pilgrimage to the Lincolnshire beach that she had loved visiting on her own childhood holidays. The East coast resort seems to get more charmingly broken down every year. She rejoices in the dilapidated wooden beach huts with their flaking paint, and the old-fashioned cafes with weather-beaten signs and their scent of candy floss, hamburgers and fish and chips. Jenny still finds so much joy in the down-at-heel amusement arcades with their aged one-armed bandits, creaking penny falls and pinball machines from a bygone age. She even loves seeing the tacky gift shops, some of which are just about clinging on against the tide, while others have already been boarded up.

Every sharp gust of blustery August wind takes her back a couple of decades to happy afternoons spent huddling behind the windbreak, with Dad in his second best suit and Mum clad in a plastic raincoat, each with a hand on a pole to stop their canvas shelter from blowing away. Jenny and her older siblings would sit or crouch on the slightly too small tartan rug, clutching their sandy sandwiches and cans of warm fizzy drink. All adorned in towels and shivering in their swimming costumes, they would train their gazes on the sky, straining to spot a gap in the heavy clouds - so desperate to seize the chance of a quick dip in the sea once the drizzle let up a little.

Story Telling Six

Sitting on the familiar beach now beside her nonplussed husband, who has finally insisted that they will be going to Spain next year, Jenny keeps a close eye on their children playing nearby. The twins seem to be quite happy looking for shells at the water's edge, each with their own pink bucket, trying to find bigger or prettier ones than her sister, to bring back to show off to their mum. The boys are building something strange in the sand while simultaneously intent on digging the deepest hole possible. Once their sand creation has collapsed, one of them is sure to end up down in the hole's cold wetness, either laughing or crying.

Turning her freckled face to the sun, Jenny reflects that she would love to lay down her flask of tea, discard the carefully-prepared picnic, cast off her sensible cardigan and strip down to her bikini. She imagines herself hurtling headlong in hysterics towards the sea, trampling on any over-elaborate sandcastles, hurdling bewildered families, kicking sand over bright red sunbathers, and startling a pensioner or two by knocking over their deckchairs. Playing out gay abandon in her mind, Jenny behaves wildly in her own inimitable style for a while. As the moment passes with the return of cloud cover, she settles for a little giggle, a private wiggle, snuggle, and a secret smile as she pours orange squash into plastic cups.

Copyright Richard Seal 2018

**

A Scottish Golf Story

John, who lived in the north of England, decided to go golfing in Scotland with his buddy, Shawn. They loaded up John's minivan and headed north. After driving for a few hours, they got caught in a terrible blizzard. So they pulled into a nearby farm and asked the attractive lady who answered the door if they could spend the night.

'I realize it's terrible weather out there and I have this huge house all to myself, but I'm recently widowed,' she explained, 'and I'm afraid the neighbors will talk if I let you stay in my house.'

'Don't worry,' John said. 'We'll be happy to sleep in the barn And if the weather breaks, we'll be gone at first light.'

The lady agreed, and the two men found

their way to the barn and settled in for the night.

Come morning, the weather had cleared, and they got on their way. They enjoyed a great weekend of golf. But about nine months later, John got an unexpected letter from an attorney. It took him a few minutes to figure it out, but he finally determined that it was from the attorney of that attractive widow he had met on the golf weekend.

He dropped in on his friend Shawn and asked, "Shawn, do you remember that good-looking widow from the farm we stayed at on our golf holiday in Scotland about 9 months ago?"

'Yes, I do,' said Shawn. 'Did you, er, happen to get up in the middle of the night, go up to the house and pay her a visit?'

'Well, um, yes!,' Shawn said, a little

embarrassed about being found out, 'I have to admit that I did.'

'And did you happen to give her my name instead of telling her your name?'

Shawn's face turned beet red and he said, 'Yeah, look, I'm sorry, buddy I'm afraid I did Why do you ask?'

'She just died and left me everything.'
**

Politicians are the same all over. They promise to build bridges even when there are no rivers. Nikita Khrushchev
**

Our elections are free...it is the results where we eventually pay. Bill Stern (U.S. Actor)
**

In general, the art of government consists of taking as much money as possible from one party of the citizens to give to the other. Voltaire (1764)

And Finally Lexophile'

a word used to describe those that have a love for words, such as "you can tune a piano, but you can't tuna fish", or "to write with a broken pencil is pointless." A competition to see who can come up with the best 'Lexophile' is held every year at an undisclosed location.

This year's winning submission is posted at the very end.

... When fish are in schools, they sometimes take debate.

... A thief who stole a calendar got twelve months.

... When the smog lifts in Los Angeles U.C.L.A.

... The batteries were given out free of charge.

... A dentist and a manicurist married They fought tooth and nail.

... A will is a dead giveaway.

... With her marriage, she got a new name and a dress.

... When you've seen one shopping center you've seen a mall.

... A boiled egg is hard to beat.

... Did you hear about the fellow whose entire left side was cut off? He's all right now.

... A bicycle can't stand alone; it's just two tired.

... I met this man playing Dancing Queen on a didgeridoo and I thought 'That's Aboriginal.'

... The guy who fell onto an upholstery machine is now fully recovered.

... He had a photographic memory which was never developed.

... Acupuncture is a jab well done. That's the point of it.

... This lorry full of tortoises collided with a van full of terrapins. It was a turtle disaster.

The wining Lexophile

... Those who get too big for their pants will be totally exposed in the end.

ALWAYS LAUGH WHEN YOU CAN; IT'S CHEAP MEDICINE!

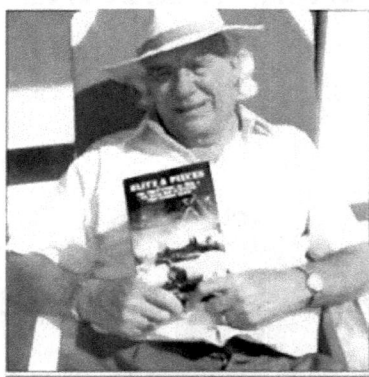

Percy W. Chattey

www.percychatteybooks.com

www.ingramcontent.com/pod-product-compliance
Lightning Source LLC
Chambersburg PA
CBHW060521030426
42337CB00015B/1959